AF469190

Mr. Marshal's Flower Album

from The Royal Library at Windsor Castle

Mr. Marshal's Flower Album

from The Royal Library at Windsor Castle

Introduction and commentary by
John Fisher

Preface by Jane Roberts
Curator of the Print Room,
The Royal Library, Windsor Castle

Victor Gollancz Limited
London 1985

First published in Great Britain in 1985
by Victor Gollancz Limited
14 Henrietta Street London WC2E 8QJ

British Library Cataloguing in Publication Data
Fisher, John, *1909–*
Mr Marshal's flower album: paintings from the
Royal Library, Windsor.
1. Marshal, Alexander
I. Title II. Marshal, Alexander
759.2 ND497.M3

ISBN 0-575-03536-6

Designed by Harold Bartram
Filmset by BAS Printers Limited,
Over Wallop, Hampshire
Printed in Italy by Imago Publishing Ltd

Contents

Acknowledgements

These notes could never have been written but for the help and encouragement of the Staff of The Royal Library at Windsor Castle – in particular from Jane Roberts whose patience and forbearance in the face of continuous visits to the Library have been exemplary.

Generous assistance – as always – has been forthcoming from the Librarian at the Lindley Library, Dr Brent Elliott and from his Assistant, Miss Barbara Collecott, to whom I am especially indebted. The Staff of the British Museum (Natural History) Library were able to dispel doubts as to the identity of seventeenth-century French nurserymen, and the Hammersmith Public Library were kind enough to show me valuable documents relating to Bishop Compton, patron and plant collector, in whose Palace at Fulham, Alexander Marshal lived for some years.

In the Library of the Royal Society I was allowed to examine the original record of the letter received from Alexander Marshal explaining, in part, the mysteries of water-colour painting, and the London Library gave access to a number of works to be seen elsewhere only with difficulty – in particular a number of seventeenth-century dictionaries of the French language. I am also grateful to Mr William Drummond for the illustrations on p. 11, and guidance on the technique used by Marshal when painting on wood. I am grateful to Miss Ann Hoffmann for her researches into records some of which were seriously depleted by the Great Fire of September 1666. My grateful thanks go to Mr E. F. Allen, Member of the Council of the Royal National Rose Society and one of its Past Presidents, and to Mrs Allen for their kindness in examining Marshal's portraits of roses and for their perceptive comments, some of which I have quoted.

The Monks' Riddle, suggested by *Rosa centifolia*, is reproduced by permission of the Hamlyn Publishing Group Ltd from *Old Garden Roses* by E. A. Bunyard – originally published by Country Life; and the singular merit of Henbane, expounded by the seventeenth-century naturalist John Ray, is quoted from Ray's *Flora of Cambridgeshire*, translated from the Latin by A. H. Ewen and the late C. T. Prime, by permission of the publishers Weldon & Wesley Ltd, of Hitchin, Hertfordshire. The illustration on p. 10 is published by permission of the Victoria and Albert Museum, and on p. 17 by permission of the Library, Academy of Natural Sciences, Philadelphia.

Finally, I am especially appreciative of the kindness and generosity of Dr Helen Brock in allowing me to make use of the penetrating researches which she has prepared for her book on the Guernsey Lily.

J.F.

In addition to my husband and to John Fisher, I am indebted to the following for their help and advice on the compilation of the Preface: Mary Beal, Helen Brock, William Drummond, Paul Hulton, Prudence Leith-Ross, Henrietta McBurney, James Mears, James Miller, John Murdoch, Jim Murrell, Francis Russell and Nicholas Turner.

J.R.

Preface

'I know an Ingenious gentleman, who this way hath made all his colours for plants, which he hath drawn to the life in a large volume of the most beautiful flours of all sorts in their proper and genuine colour.'

C. Merret, *The Art of Glass* (1662)

Marshal's exquisite paintings of flowers, the subject of this book and almost certainly the subject of the quotation above, were the product of the great revival of interest in natural history following the Renaissance, which inspired a large number of illustrations of flowers and plants, birds, animals and insects. Their distant antecedents can be found in the border decorations of illuminated manuscripts, and in medieval herbals, which considered the practical rather than the beautiful aspects of flowers and plants.

The Low Countries, in which the cultivation of flowers (above all, tulips) reached fever-pitch in the mid-seventeenth century, produced many brilliant botanical artists, both in oils and in water-colour, but the main developments in botanical illustration were made in France, where Nicolas Robert (1614–85) was commissioned to paint the flowers and animals at Blois for Louis XIII's younger brother, Gaston d'Orléans. Robert was also involved at an early stage with the work of the Académie Royale des Sciences, and was chosen as chief illustrator for their planned history of plants.

The Académie Royale was the French equivalent of the Royal Society in London, founded in 1660 after a series of weekly meetings from 1645 onwards by 'divers worthy persons, inquisitive into natural philosophy and other parts of human learning'. The same climate which produced and fostered the foundation of the Royal Society also encouraged the early English botanists, and it was in England that the most important contributions were made to that science during the seventeenth century. These botanists nurtured, introduced, described and recorded their plants, but few of the resulting *Florilegia* have survived for posterity. Alexander Marshal, the painter of the Windsor *Florilegium*, therefore stands virtually alone at this time in the history of English botanical art.

Marshal's date of birth remains unknown, but it is known that he died at Fulham Palace, the seat of the Bishop of London, on 7th December 1682, leaving a widow, Dorothea (daughter of Francis Smith), but no children. The administration of his Will was granted to Dorothea on 3rd January 1683; her Will, dated 30th July 1711 with a codicil of 14th September 1711, was proved on 2nd October 1711. However, the discovery of a number of the artist's insect studies and notes now in Philadelphia, and the researches of Prudence Leith-Ross into the papers of Samuel Hartlib, an educationalist of Marshal's day, have yielded much new information.

Marshal first appears as a mature artist in the late 1640s, and was probably therefore born before 1625. According to Hartlib, he was previously a merchant, resident for some time in France. The French names used for some of the plants in the Windsor *Florilegium* and in the inscription (entirely in French) on the reverse of Marshal's miniature of the *Countess of Dysart* (painted in 1649), would seem to support this claim, as would a reference to Vespasien Robin, royal gardener in Paris, to whom Marshal sent a sword-fly. It is tempting to suggest that while in France Marshal may have encountered Nicolas Robert. The layout of Marshal's flowers on the page is at times very similar to that of Robert's *Diverses Fleurs*, published in 1640. Dr Mear's study of the insect drawings (now in Philadelphia) has led him to suggest that Marshal also visited South America. These drawings include notes such as 'observation I made when I was [in] Rio de La Platta . . .'.

More relevant to the Windsor *Florilegium* is the fact that, according to Hartlib, Marshal was one of the greatest florists (i.e. growers of plants) of his day, and an agriculturalist and collector of birds and insects. Marshal's great-nephew and eventual heir, William Freind, described him as a gentleman with 'an independent fortune [who] painted merely for his Amusement'. The inscriptions to Marshal's natural historical drawings are the product of a well-educated mind, being in both Latin and English, and in one instance in Greek.

Already in 1658 Marshal was described in Sir William Sanderson's *Graphice* as a flower and fruit artist, among 'Our Modern Masters comparable with any now beyond seas'. He was thus one of a large number of 'gentleman artists', particularly limners (water-colourists), active in England in the seventeenth century, capable of remarkably competent works of art, for whom any financial reward was of little consequence. Another amateur artist, John Lambert, was the son of General Lambert, who presented Marshal with the Guernsey lily in 1659, and was described by Walpole and others as 'a great encourager of painting and a good performer in flowers'.

Marshal's first surviving dated work, the miniature of the *Countess of Dysart* of 1649, was recently acquired for the Victoria and Albert Museum and is now at Ham House, near Richmond in Surrey. This is a copy of an original by Hoskins of 1638, but replacing the landscape background with a view of Ham House itself.

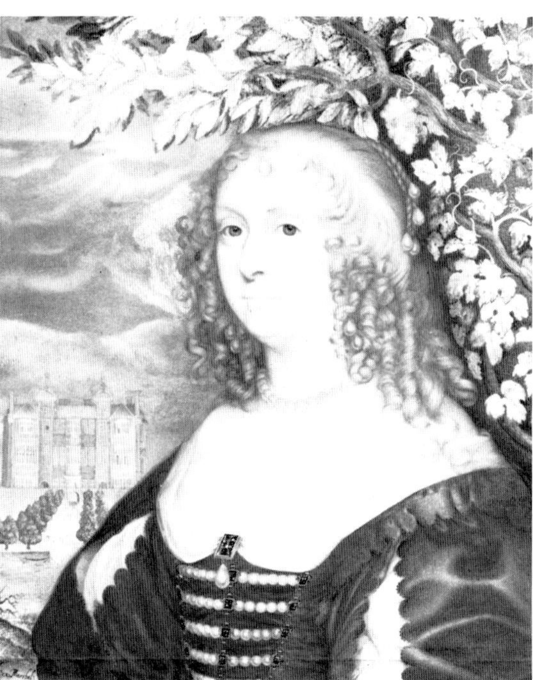

In 1650 Hartlib noted that Marshal resided at Ham with 'a whole chamber of insects which make a glorious representation'. He adds that Marshal (whom he was not to meet until 1654) was 'very skilful in drawing painting and representing of anything', and that John Tradescant owned a book by Marshal 'very lively representing most of the things' in his garden. The *Countess of Dysart* miniature by Marshal is in a standard limner's technique, closely resembling the original. Furthermore, Marshal's portrait, like Hoskins', was applied to plain (not gessoed) card, which might suggest that Marshal received tuition in limning from Hoskins or from a member of his studio.

There are several dated works from the 1650s consisting mostly of copies after Van Dyck and earlier masters. But the two surviving flower panels also date from this time. The *Swag of Flowers*, dated 1652, and painted in distemper on panel,

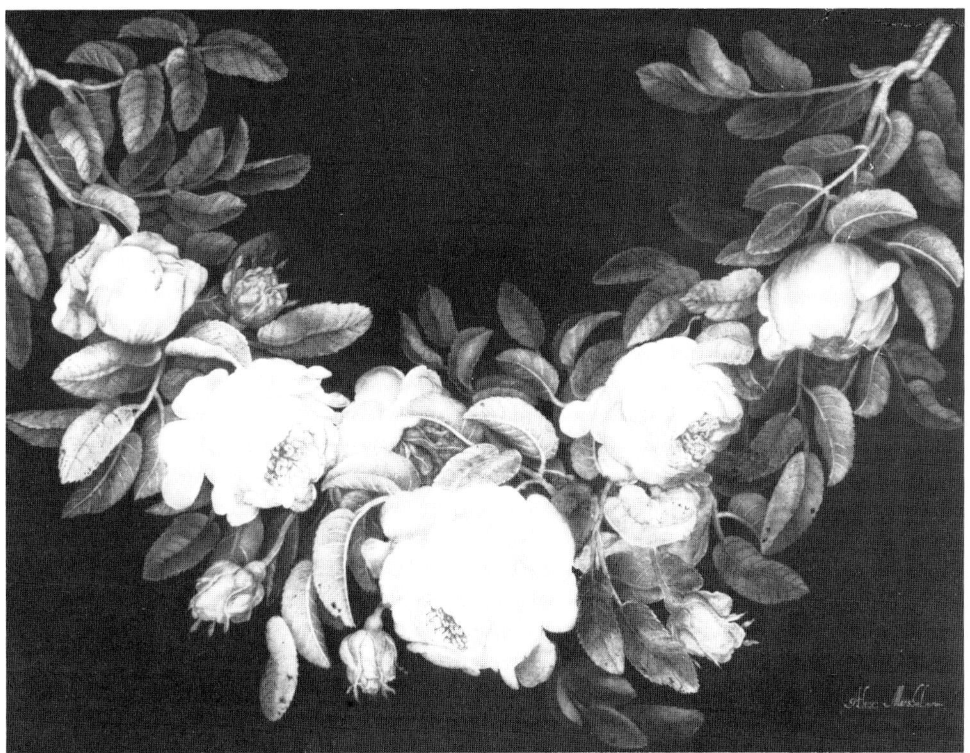

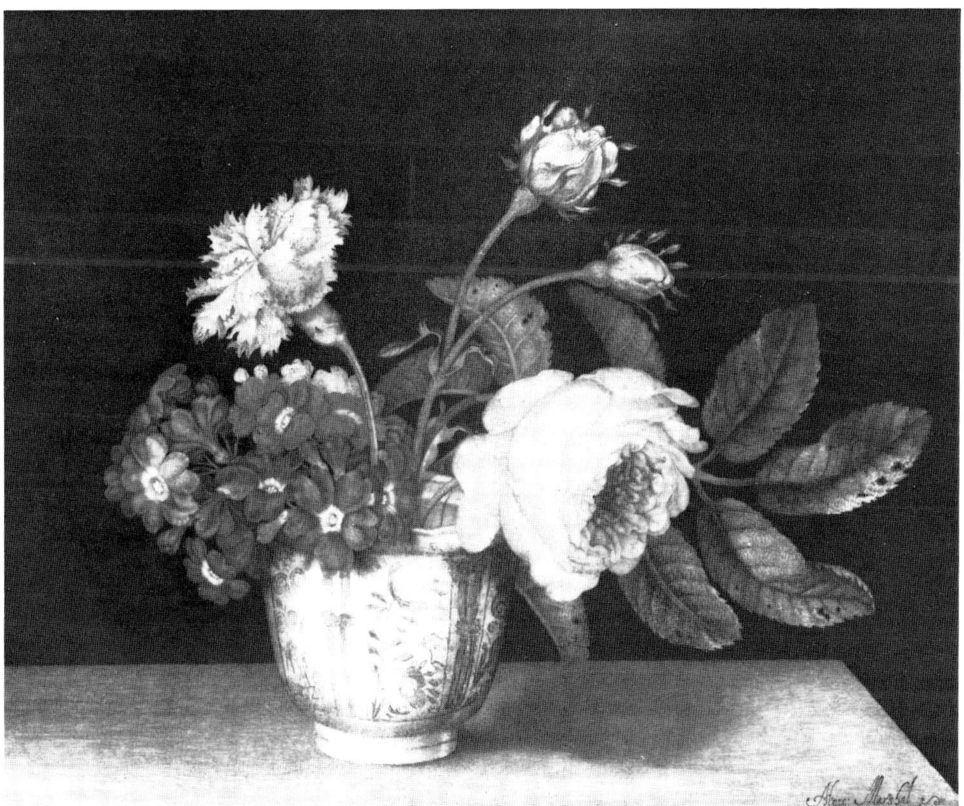

is untypical of Marshal's work, first for its size, which is considerably larger than his other works, and secondly for its *raison d'être*. It seems to have belonged to a series of *trompe l'œil* swags which would have formed part of the decoration of a room. The exquisite picture of *Flowers in a Delft Jar* at Yale (in oil on panel) probably also dates from these years. (It is dated, but illegibly.)

The only letter in Marshal's hand that has so far come to light is one addressed to Sir Justice Isham, now in the Northamptonshire Record Office. It is inscribed 'London, 6 August 1651,' and refers to a recent meeting with 'My Lord, of

Northampton'. The artist's connection with the Northampton/Compton family was therefore of long standing. His letter to the Royal Society, dated November 1667, was written from Castle Ashby, seat of James, the 3rd Earl of Northampton, and Marshal spent the last years of his life in Fulham Palace, home of the 3rd Earl's brother, Henry Compton, who was Bishop of London from 1675. It appears that Marshal had no house of his own. Apart from his sojourns with various members of the Compton family, he is mentioned as living at Ham in 1650, London in 1651, and Islington in 1654 where he resided with the son of an Alderman Dewes (or Dawes). Hartlib also records that Marshal cultivated a garden at the Earl of Northampton's (i.e. at any of their houses, which included one in Islington). By 1667, Marshal claimed that he was 'giving over water colours finding it tedious and forcible to the eyes', and intended to practise in oil instead. It is curious that the surviving oil painting by Marshal is the flower panel done in the 1650s.

Most of Marshal's surviving work is inevitably and intentionally derivative. Some paintings evidently depended on originals in his own collection, including prints which (like the Windsor *Florilegium*) later passed to the Freind family. Although a number of portrait miniatures by Marshal are listed in early sources (Vertue, the Freind catalogue and sale catalogue, etc.), the only one that has so far come to light is an extraordinarily unattractive portrait in plumbago of a child aged twenty-nine weeks, signed and dated 1653, a work which suggests that Marshal may not have excelled as a portraitist.

It is instead in Marshal's activity as a painter of natural history that his true artistic talent and ingenuity are displayed. His collection of insects was already noted by Hartlib in 1650, and was recorded by Evelyn in 1682. Marshal was a keen lepidopterist and seems to have enlisted the help of both Tradescant, and Bishop Compton and his chaplains in distant parts, in acquiring many rare insects. Captain Thomas Roe returned from the Barbados with a beetle for Marshal. Captain Chamberlain brought him two sword flies from Ethiopia. Captain Stains brought him a locust from Hispagnola, Sir Henry Moody sent him a Harlequin Beetle from America, and Mr Punic gave him a lantern moth he had received from a brother resident in India. Some of the insects, such as the cerampids caught in Warwickshire in 1667, were evidently collected at home. Elsewhere Marshal recorded breeding a caterpillar and feeding it on willow leaves.

Marshal must have been well established as a flower painter by the 1640s when John Tradescant commissioned from him the (now lost) 'Booke of . . . choicest Flowers and Plants, exquisitely limned in vellum'; these words describe the volume in the *Musaeum Tradescantium* (1656), but it had also been noted by Hartlib in 1650.

The Windsor *Florilegium* is almost certainly identifiable with the 'curious book of flowers in miniature' which John Evelyn saw at Fulham Palace on 1st August 1682. The wording of the passage in which Evelyn records this visit is crucial. The diarist wrote that he visited Fulham 'to review the additions which Mr. Marshall had made to his curious book of flowers . . .', thus implying that the book was a progressive accumulation rather than a work of one or two years. Indeed it may have been compiled over a number of years, for he notes on his painting of the Guernsey Lily that it 'was sent me by Generall Lambert august 29 1659 fro[m] Wimbleton'. The 'flower' could have included a root which, if successfully transplanted, may have survived for some years. But this particular plant was then found to be very difficult to keep and nurture, and it is more than likely that Marshal painted it soon after August 1659. On another plate a bird is described as 'a Indian fowll w[hich] was presented to the Pr[ince] of orenge'. This may have been one of the New Year's gifts which the future King William III received during his visit to England in 1670/71 (at which time he certainly met Henry Compton, then canon of Christ Church Oxford): 'twenty English horses, besides deer and rare birds for his parks and aviaries'. On another plate a plant is described as 'the trew figure of Ginger as it grew at Fulham' (see p. 107); Marshal's connection with Fulham depended on his friendship with Henry Compton, who only resided there from 1675, the year of his appointment as Bishop of London.

In 1667 Marshal himself refers to a particular book of his paintings in the Royal Society letter: 'The search of colours has cost me much time in finding out, and to know, which would hold colour in water, and mix well; else I had not used them in my book.' The work that went into the Windsor *Florilegium* is prodigious by any standards, particularly so when the amount of time and trouble involved in the making of each special colour is considered. It is Marshal's outstanding surviving work: the book into which he poured all his botanical and artistic interest, from the late 1650s to the time of his death in 1682.

The history of the Windsor *Florilegium* since Marshal's death in 1682 is known in all but a few details. In spite of an offer of £500 on behalf of Louis XIV, the artist's widow, Dorothea, bequeathed the album to her sister's son, Robert Freind (1667–1751), who became headmaster of Westminster School. Robert Freind in turn bequeathed it to his son, William (1715–66), Dean of Canterbury, who was responsible for the catalogue now in the British Museum. (The description of the *Florilegium* in this catalogue is informative on many counts, and has therefore been included here as Appendix B.

After William Freind's death, the album was included, as lot 46, in the sale of the 'Valuable and much esteemed Museum of the late Rev. Dr. Freind' on 25th April 1777 at Christie's in London, where it was purchased by a Mr Way for £52 10s. 0d.

The subsequent fate of the *Florilegium* can be traced from the inscriptions repeated at the beginning of the two volumes as they exist today: they were purchased in Brussels for John Mangles (of Hurley, Berkshire) by his friend Ross Donelly in 1818.

The date of the breaking up of the original album may have been very recent, for the paper of the Index to Volume I (which was presumably made at the time of the rebinding) bears a watermark 'J. Whatman 1811'. Mangles signed and dated his introductory remarks 27th April 1820, and at some subsequent (but unrecorded) date presented the two volumes to King George IV.

The freshness of the paintings in the Windsor album is truly remarkable, and must result from the fact that they have not been exposed to light. Many contemporary sources testify to the artist's interest in colour. Samuel Hartlib saw Marshal in 1650 as a 'new man of Experiments and Art'. Soon after the foundation of the Royal Society in 1660, Marshal was approached by Thomas Povey to advise on the different painting techniques then in use; other artists were also approached, including Lely, Cooper and Streeter, all three of whom agreed to collaborate. However, Marshal felt unable to do so, and on 30th November 1667 wrote to Povey:

> 'Sir, I had answered yours, had it come to my hands sooner, I am very willing to satisfy in part your desire concerning my colours, but how to express the handling of them I know not, for practice puts me in a new way every day. One colour may set out the other by composition or transparence, which leaves the beauty, as the flower or other things require. I thought seven years ago that I knew much, but I find, that practice shews me daily more than I knew before; but the last week I tried one colour, and calcined it in three several pots, and in one fire together, the pots being cold, I found in them three several colours, which was but one at first, the one was red, the other yellow, and the other amber, and all very good for use. As for the colours I make out of flowers, or berries, or gums, or roots, they are more subtle, and have not so great a body, as minerals, which I turn into lakes, or dry them in shells, which I temper with such waters, as I make fit for them and my use. The search of colours has cost me much time in finding out, and to know, which would hold colour in water, and mix well; else I had not used them in my book; and am sure, will be as fresh a hundred years hence, as when you saw them last. The truth is, they are pretty secrets, but known, they are nothing. Several have been at me to know, how; as if they were but trifles, and not worth secrecy. To part with them as yet I desire to be excused. I have in a manner given over water-colours, finding it tedious

and forcible to the eyes, which has put me upon the practice in oil, and I am in good hopes, that my colours will shew themselves as beautiful in oil as water, though many will say, that it is needless for oil-colours to be so orient or beautiful in painting. In my opinion 'tis a great prejudice to painters also, to paint carelessly with any colours, that will starve, and become nothing, by a salt, that is in them. Certainly Brueigeelh and Elshmer, and other masters, had a way in cleansing and curing their colours, which as yet is to be seen in their small curious works as fresh as ever they were, for salt and oil cannot agree long, and so were parted by those masters, that their fame might last as well for their colours as work. Sir, I beg your pardon, not knowing whether my abrupt discourse does answer your desire; and so I rest, Sir, Your humble and most obliged Servant

Alex Marshal'

As a botanist, Marshal was ideally placed to have access to a wide variety of plant juices to make the colours for his paints. William Freind's introductory account notes that Marshal 'is said to have had a particular art of extracting Colors out of the Natural Flowers; and some of the Plants and Flowers contained in this Volume are painted with those colors. This secret, though left behind him, died with those to whom he intrusted it:' No scientific analysis has yet been carried out on the paints used in the Windsor album, but the wide range of colours and textures achieved makes it highly likely that such analysis would reveal much use of plant-derived dyes. Comparison between the colours of the foliage in Hoskins' original of the *Countess of Dysart*, and in Marshal's copy, with vivid greens in the former, and residual yellows and browns in the latter, suggests that Marshal's greens were here derived from plant juices, and therefore very susceptible to the fading effects of light. The use of plant juices and other natural substances to extend the artist's colour range had been recommended by theorists since antiquity. Marshal was not exceptional in this respect.

The sources of the other colours used in the *Florilegium* can only be guessed at. Some of the greens appear to have incorporated verdigris, whose corrosive effects were doubtless responsible for the perished paper fibres on some of the illustrations. The bright orange on two of them (not shown here) was probably created by the addition of lakes onto a ground of yellow orpiment (arsenic trisulphide). In his letter to the Royal Society Marshal describes making three colours out of one, probably referring to white lead, and its yellow, orange and red derivatives. Red lead may be seen, with its characteristic discoloration, on the red pepper on p. 107. A few tiny flecks of gold are visible on the flower of 'greekish valerian' (not shown here). Silver seems to have been used, added to gum arabic to give a varied range of shading (e.g. his paintings of the anemone and the jonquil [not shown here]).

It will probably never be possible to tell exactly how far Marshal's powers of inventiveness in the creation of new colours exceeded those of his contemporaries. In his time he was known as an 'ingenuous' (i.e. ingenious) gentleman. Marshal kept his secrets from his fellow artists and scholars, and apart from the few details rehearsed above, very little has been revealed about his life and work since his death over three hundred years ago. But for many, the pleasure of turning the pages of Marshal's *Florilegium*, and of the present volume, revealing colours of an unsurpassed vibrancy, will suffice.

Windsor
August 1984

Introduction

The period in which Marshal lived was, despite its political instability, one of great botanical activity. John Tradescant the younger had made expeditions to Virginia in 1637, 1642 and 1656. At home, John Ray, the son of an Essex blacksmith, who rose to be Junior Dean of Trinity College Cambridge, was travelling far and wide on horseback, gathering material for his synopsis of British Flora, which remained a standard work for nearly fifty years after its appearance in 1690. Edward Lloyd or Lhwyd, as he preferred it, was quartering Wales to discover the beautiful and rare Snowdon Lily which otherwise grows no nearer than the Alps.

Not even politicians were immune from plant fever. In Marshal's time, Sir Henry Capel, at one time Lord Lieutenant in Ireland, was cultivating a garden at Kew which later became the site of the Royal Botanic Gardens. Sir Thomas Hanmer, a royalist, who had prudently retired to his estate in North Wales for the duration of the Commonwealth, was growing 26 different tulips and 60 varieties of iris.

Sir Ralph Verney, another royalist, returned from exile in 1653 to tend his Persian tulips, ranunculuses, pinks and gilliflowers. General John Lambert, a leading General on the Parliamentary side – (of whom more, later) – was improving his magnificent garden at Wimbledon, and Nehemiah Grew, Secretary to the Royal Society, was observing the sexual functioning of plants, and propounding theories which led, in the next century, to the first experiments in hybridization.

The most eager horticulturalist of them all was perhaps Henry Compton (1632–1713), Bishop of London. He had been a Cornet in the Horse Guards and had probably fought both in the Civil War and in Flanders. He did not enter the Church until he was in his thirties, but through the influence of Sir Thomas Osborne, first Earl of Danby, his promotion was rapid. He became Canon of Christ Church, Oxford, in 1669, Bishop of Oxford in 1674, and Bishop of London and Dean of the Chapel Royal in 1675. He was appointed religious instructor to the two princesses both of whom were later Queens: Mary, who married William of Orange, whom he crowned, and Anne, and his strongly-held Protestant convictions thus helped to ensure that the succession to the throne remained ultimately in Protestant hands. His own career was temporarily blighted by James II, a declared Catholic who, after succeeding to the throne, dismissed Compton from the Privy Council and from his appointment as Dean of the Chapel Royal. He was also suspended – without loss of salary, however – from his duties as Bishop of London for refusing to condemn attacks on the growing influence of Catholics in public life. Small wonder, then, that he later signed the invitation to William Prince of Orange to come to England on an expedition, which led to the deposition of James II and the restoration of his own position. But gardening came very close after godliness according to his reckoning, and in Fulham he found an ideal gardening site.

John Bowack, antiquarian and Writing Master at Westminster School, described the gardens at Fulham 'very fine and entertaining', adding that the 'kindness of the soyle and great plenty of water makes them very proper for the breeding of some choice foreign plants of which there is a very valuable collection'.

In those days the grounds of the Bishop's Palace extended to the river and there were private stairs 'to take water'. The gardens and the small park adjoining them were moated all round with a long canal, well stocked with fish, on the banks of which were 'five or six choice physical [medicinal] plants not discovered to grow in any other part of England'. There were several stove houses too for the more tender immigrants and a walled garden.

Nor was Compton a passive onlooker. Stephen Switzer, who worked for George London, Compton's gardener, wrote of Compton that: 'few days a year [passed] but he was actually in his garden ordering and directing the removal and replacement of his trees and plants.'

Compton was a member of the Temple Coffee House Botanists' Club, and as spiritual head of the Church in the American colonies, was able to send a chaplain to Virginia who could recognize good exotic plants when he saw them – and send them back to his Bishop.

Compton, as we have seen, did not become Bishop of London till 1675, but almost certainly knew Marshal before then – though possibly not while the artist was preparing his album. However, Dr William Freind recalled that Marshal 'had lived for many years in great friendship with Dr Compton, and died at his Palace at Fulham.'

Thus what with the Bishop, the General, the Countess of Dysart and John Evelyn, Marshal seems to have moved in a rarefied social atmosphere. He may, conceivably, have known Izaak Walton (who was acquainted with both Tradescant and Ashmole) although Walton's views would have been anything but acceptable to any genuine botanist.

To Walton, the marigold was a flower, the colour of which was comparable to that of the skin on a trout's belly; water lilies were to be killed off at all costs by drying out the pond in which they grew; the honeysuckle hedge was something to shelter under during a summer shower, and the yellow flag iris was tolerated only because it fostered certain insects that were attractive to bream. The two men might, however, have come closer on the subject of the orange, of which Marshal successfully painted a portrait. Walton included the rinds of oranges and lemons in a mixture of claret, well seasoned with salt, cloves and mace, to be poured over a carp stuffed with oysters and anchovies. He also allowed his pupil, Venator, to offer him a draught compounded of 'a bottle of sack, milk, oranges, and sugar, which, all put together, make a drink like nectar; indeed, too good for anyone but us Anglers.'

It is not known whether Walton ever had the opportunity of making an exception in Marshal's case.

One of the mysteries that Marshal left behind him concerns the way in which the plants shown in his album were identified. Names of the plants were written on the back of the illustration, a fairly common practice among sixteenth- and seventeenth-century Dutch artists. It has always been assumed that the handwriting of these descriptions was Marshal's, particularly since one of them (folio 151) reads 'this flower was sent me by Generall Lambert on August 29th 1659 from Wimbleton'. Furthermore, two particularly stylish and elegant inscriptions on the rectos of folios 58 and 76 (shown opposite) accord closely with the formal signatures on Marshal's paintings.

However it is clear that the artist could not have written all the descriptions himself. For example, on the verso of folio 144 relating to a handsome red-flowered plant we read: 'Scarlet Coluthea or Aethiopian Bladder-Senna with scarlet flowers and leaves like the Silver Bush – Miller 4th sort under Colutea' (not shown here). This could have been written only by someone who had examined the *Gardener's Dictionary* produced by Philip Miller, the Scotsman, who, for forty-six years, was Superintendent of the Chelsea Physic Garden. His *Dictionary* appeared in 1724 – more than forty years after Marshal's death.

Many of the names given on the versos of the pages of Marshal's album show traces of French influence. Hartlib wrote that Marshal had spent some years in France and spoke the language fluently. He – Marshal – might have been among those who moved from England to the continent to avoid the disruptive atmosphere of the Civil War.

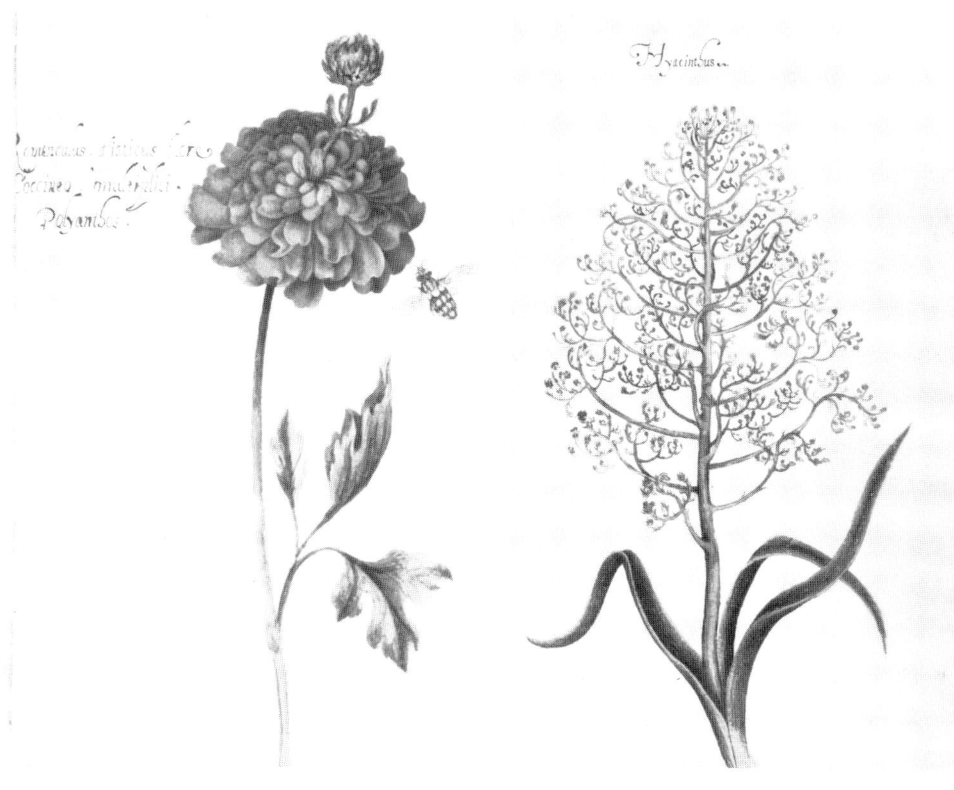

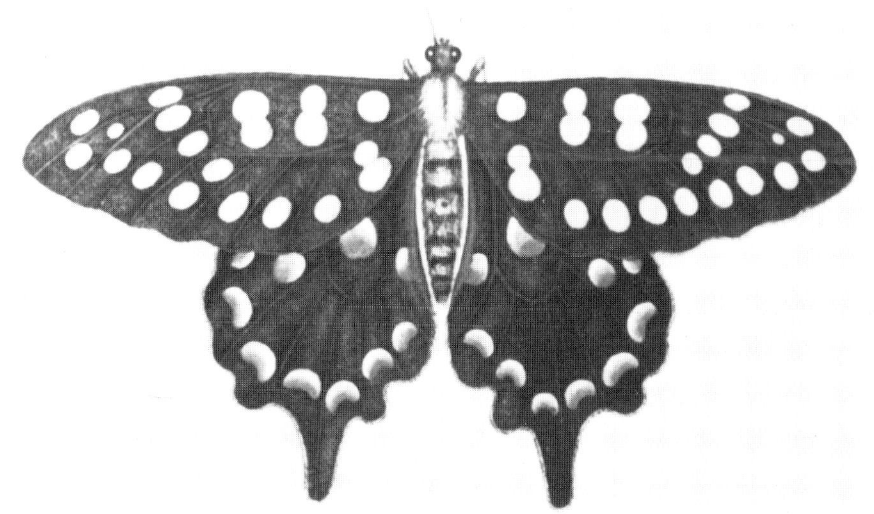

Specimens of Marshal's handwriting

But the quality of the translation is variable. For example, the tulip variety General Le Man comes out, in Marshal's handwriting, as 'Generall the Man', and, on one occasion 'pase manaque' is rendered as 'run away'. In other cases supplementary French names have been added to perfectly adequate English identifications. Thus 'read honiesockle' has beneath it the French equivalent – a slightly mis-spelled *Chevrefeuille*, and 'raged robin' has the note 'in french, cuidrelles or coucou Giliefloυer'.

These comments would have been Marshal's own, though, if he had been at all familiar with the French names for wild flowers, one would have expected more French equivalents to have appeared. Those that did so may have been the result of sporadic comments here and there by French speakers to whom Marshal showed his flower paintings – a subject to which we shall return later.

The Restoration period, in which Marshal flourished, ended in 1685 with the death of Charles II, and Marshal himself quit the scene three years earlier without, apparently, leaving readily ascertainable clues as to his origin, upbringing, education, family ties, establishment, or way of life. He was buried in All Saints church at Fulham, beneath a tombstone which read:

ALEXANDER MARSHALL
EX HONESTIA FAMILIA ORIUNDUS
DOROTHEAM FILIAM FRANCISCI
SMITH GENEROSI UXOREM DUXIT
PROLEM NON RELIQUIT AT PROBITATE
ET INGENIO LONGIOR HUIC FACTA EST
QUAM DATA VITA FUIT

OBIT DECEMBRIS 7 1682

A free translation would run:

Alexander Marshall
descended from an honourable family
married Dorothea, daughter of Francis
Smith of noble birth. He left no progeny
but, through his honesty and talents, he
will outlive the life that was granted to him.

He died on December 7th 1682

The church was re-built in 1880 and, when efforts were made to remove the stone, it fell to pieces. But the prophecy which Bishop Compton might well have caused to be engraved on the memorial to his friend was amply fulfilled.

The Flower Album

In each group of names in the section that follows those in bold type are taken from the index placed at the beginning of each volume of Marshal's album. The names in italic are taken from the verso of the album pages. Where no evidence to the contrary is shown, it is assumed that Marshal himself provided the information leading to the identification of the plants which he had painted.

Winter Aconite

Wolfes bane Winter
acognites hiemalle
the winter woolfes bane

It seems that Marshal decided to begin his sketchbook at the beginning of the year, and that at the outset no suitable flowers were to hand. At any rate most of page one and a part of page two are devoted to studies of dogs. There are wolf-hounds grey and brown, poodles, evidently used as in France as gun-dogs and close shorn to allow them to pass unhindered through bramble thickets, grizzled hounds suitable for stag-hunting, guard-dogs, hungry-looking with no spare fat on their ribs, and, apparently unmoved, a fox, alert but sitting, its brush wrapped round its body.

On the second page, also, there is a dog, but with it flowers, one of which shown here is *Eranthis hyemalis*, the Winter Aconite, which can be expected to flower as early as January in the south of England. It is an introduced plant that has become naturalized in woods and parks, and there is usually a fine show of them by the moat beneath the Round Tower in Windsor Castle, close by the Royal Library in which Marshal's paintings are treasured.

Each of the plant's stems carries at the end a single bowl of gold, formed by the sepals, and, beneath the bowl, lies a green bib, a whorl of three stalkless leaves. The flowers are highly sensitive to changes in temperature and open almost at once as soon as the thermometer shows 10°C.

The flowers are pollinated by bees and flies and, presumably, when the temperature is below ten degrees, there is less chance of the insects visiting them.

Gerard has a graphic description of this plant: 'whose leaues come forth of the groand in the dead time of winter, many times bearing the snow vpon their heads of his leaues and floures; yea the colder the weather is, the lesser is the floure, and worse coloured: these leaues I say come forth of the ground immediatly from the root, with a naked, soft, and slender stem, deeply cut or iagged on the leaues, of an exceeding fair greene colour, in the midst of which commeth forth a yellow floure, in shew or fashion like vnto the common field Crow-foot: after which follow sundry cods full of browne seeds like the other kindes of Aconites: the root is thicke, tuberous, and knottie, like to the kindes of Anemone . . . . It groweth vpon the mountaines of Germany: we haue great quantitie of it in our London gardens . . .

'This herbe is counted to be very dangerous and deadly, hot and drie in the fourth degree, as *Theoph* [Theophrastus] in plaine words doth testifie concerning his owne Aconite; for which he saith that there was never found his Antidote or remedie: whereof *Athenaus* and *Theopompus* write, that this plant is the most poisonous herb of all others . . . notwithstanding it is not without his peculiar vertues. *Ioachimus Camerarius* now liuing in Noremberg saith, the water dropped into the eies ceaseth the pain and burning: it is reported to preuaile mightily against the bitings of scorpions, and is of such force, that if the scorpion passe by where it groweth and touch the same, presently he becommeth dull, heauy, and sencelesse, and if the same scorpion chance touch the white Hellebor, he is presently deliuered from his drowsinesse.'

The true aconite, the blue-flowered Monk's Hood, is a native plant and does not bloom until May or June. But it has something in common with Winter Aconite. Both plants contain an alkaloid poison which, in the case of the Monk's Hood, was used, in small quantities, by monks and apothecaries for alleviating tooth-ache.

Winter Aconite is shown on the top right

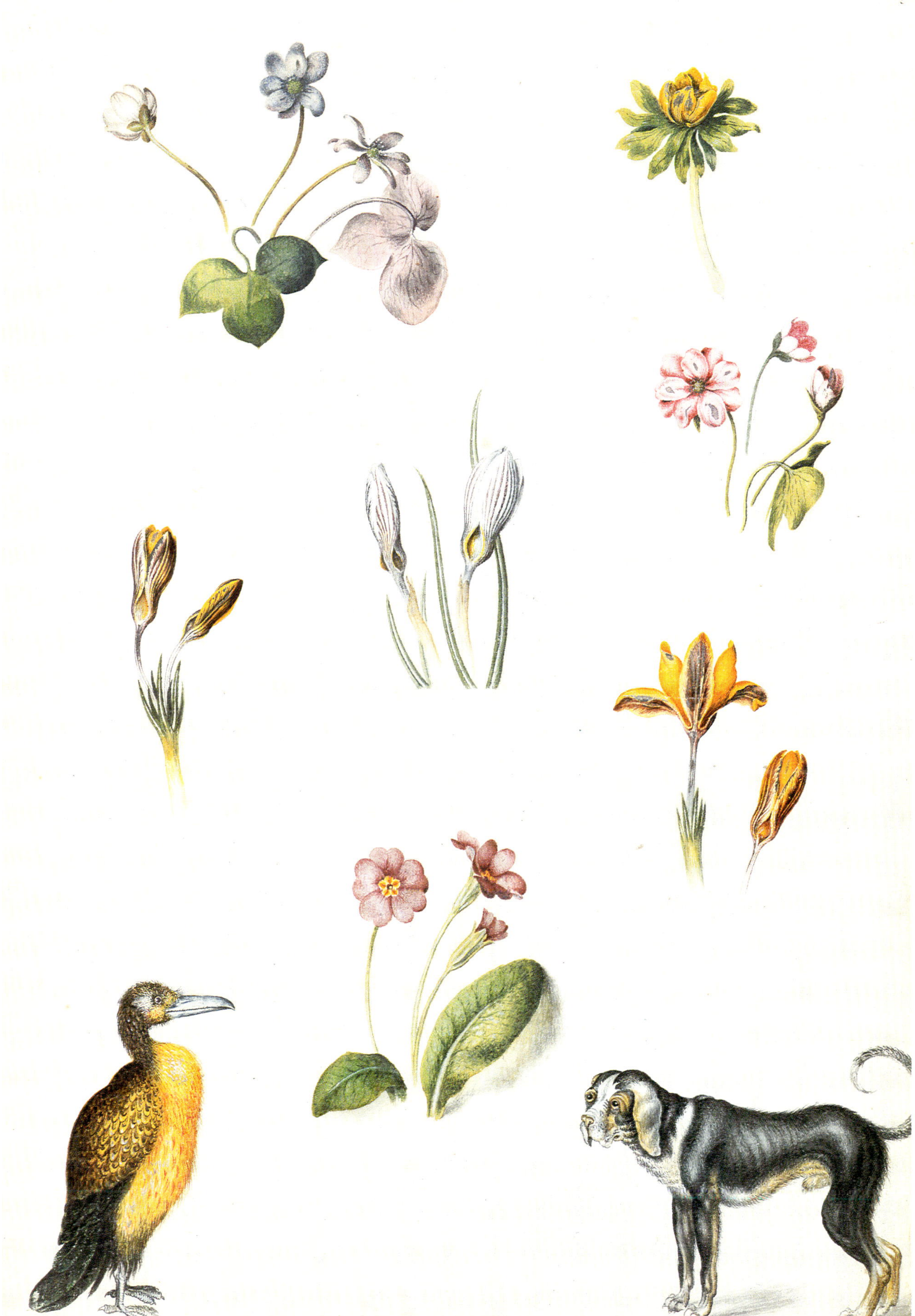

Liverwort

Liverwort noble tricolor
hepatica nobilis sive trifolia
noble Liuerworth
and
Liverworth, double red
hepatica flore rubro
read hepatica or noble Liverworth

These are nothing to do with the non-flowering liverworts of modern botany – and everything to do with the spring, as one can see from the fact that they are painted on the same page as the Winter Aconite. These are noble liverworts with trifoliate leaves like the trefoil with which Gerard confused them.

They used once to be called anemones (even by Linnaeus), but now the experts have changed back to the name Marshal used, *Hepatica*. The species was named at a time when the plant was valued more as a herb than as an ornament. The shape of the leaves reminded the surgeons of the shape of a human liver – so the plant had to be good for liver complaints.

Liverwort is shown on the top left and mid right of p.21

Hepatica nobilis, sometimes called *H. trifolia*, or even *H. triloba*, is at home in America and Asia as well as in Europe and has many different colour forms, but the indexer seems to have nodded off when he called it 'tricolor'.

Crocus

Crocus, Cloth of Silver
crocus albus versicolor
Cloth of Silver

Crocus, Cloth of Gold
Crocus vernus Luteus versicolor primus
Dur Crocus, or the best Cloath of gold

The first of these two crocuses had earlier been known as 'The Lesser Party Coloured White Crocus' because of the 'blew strakes' on the white flower, but Parkinson in his *Paradisi in Sole Paradisus Terrestris* (1629) does not dignify it with any other title. He agrees however that the second crocus deserves the name 'Best Cloth of Gold Crocus'. It 'riseth up very early', is distinguished by its whitish leaves and gives rise to pale golden flowers, striped with 'faire and great stripes'.

Parkinson's Cloth of Silver Crocus was a different plant altogether: *Crocus vernus versicolor albidoluteus*, the flowers of which are the colour of winter butter and are striped with pale purple. It was the last of twenty-seven spring crocuses which he described.

The crocuses are shown on p.21, centre

Primrose

Primrose, single red
primula veris
primrose

This could be the form which replaces our own yellow primrose in parts of Greece, Turkey and the Caucasus. Parkinson described it as 'Tradescant's purple Turkie primrose', and Marshal could very well have obtained it from Tradescant whose plants, as we have seen, he had painted on another occasion on vellum.

The authoritative *Flora of the British Isles* (1962 edition) says of our own wild primrose: 'Cultivated forms with pink or white flowers are sometimes found growing in hedges and the pink form in woods in Wales, where it may be native.' However the comprehensive work, *The Flowering Plants of Wales* (1984) is mute on this point.

The Primrose is shown on p.21, bottom centre

Since Marshal's day, the cowslip has become *Primula veris*, and the primrose, *Primula vulgaris*.

The Orange

Orange
Mala Arantia
orange

The name 'orange' had been in use in English since the fifteenth century, but originally called a 'norange' from the Spanish 'naranja'.

This 'golden apple' could have reached Marshal from General Lambert – for there was an orangery at the Manor of Wimbledon. Or it could have originated from Sir Thomas Hanmer. Hanmer, at the time he wrote his *Garden Book*, described the orange tree thus: 'at the foot of each leaf is the shape of a little heart, upon which the leaf stands,' which distinguishes the orange from the lemon – a feature to which Marshal paid some attention. Hanmer considered that there were 20 different kinds of orange in Italy and from his own description he was well-acquainted with both the Sweet and Seville Orange as well as with the 'Bermuda' Orange or Shaddock, the ancestor of the modern grapefruit. All three species came from the Far East as Miles Hadfield points out in his invaluable *A History of British Gardening*. The Sweet Orange, more or less correctly labelled as the Chinese Orange, came from China or Indochina, as did the Seville Orange; and the Shaddock, named after a Captain Shaddock, originated probably in Malaysia.

Having regard to the climate of their country, most horticulturalists grew orange trees not so much for the fruit as for their neat foliage and sweet-smelling flowers and leaves. But to fulfil even these more modest ambitions the plants had to be kept under cover through the winter months.

In one of the earliest orangeries at Beddington, near Croydon, the trees were planted in open ground, and covered during the autumn and winter by wooden 'sentry-boxes' warmed by stoves. But at the Manor of Wimbledon, which was surveyed in detail in 1649 by the Parliamentary Commissioners, the orange trees were grown in boxes and transferred to a sheltered position during the colder months.

The early fanciers sought to save time by importing ready-grown orange trees, but the journey from Italy or even France seemed to weaken them, and Hanmer resorted to growing them from seed. It was, however, a laborious operation. The seeds had first to be sown in seed-boxes and well watered. When they had taken they were singled out and transferred to pots of the kind used for carnations or stocks. There they would remain for three or four years until they grew too large. They were then moved in the spring into wooden cases, well-jointed at the seams and provided with holes at the bottom for drainage. Although these cases were a yard high, in the long run they would not prove large enough, and every three or four years the trees would have to be taken out, the roots pruned, and the trees replaced in a more spacious container.

Both the crocuses shown lower on the page are described as 'crocus, deep purple'; and the Grass snake, lifting its head in readiness perhaps to eat the cockchafer larva beneath, is described as 'English'.

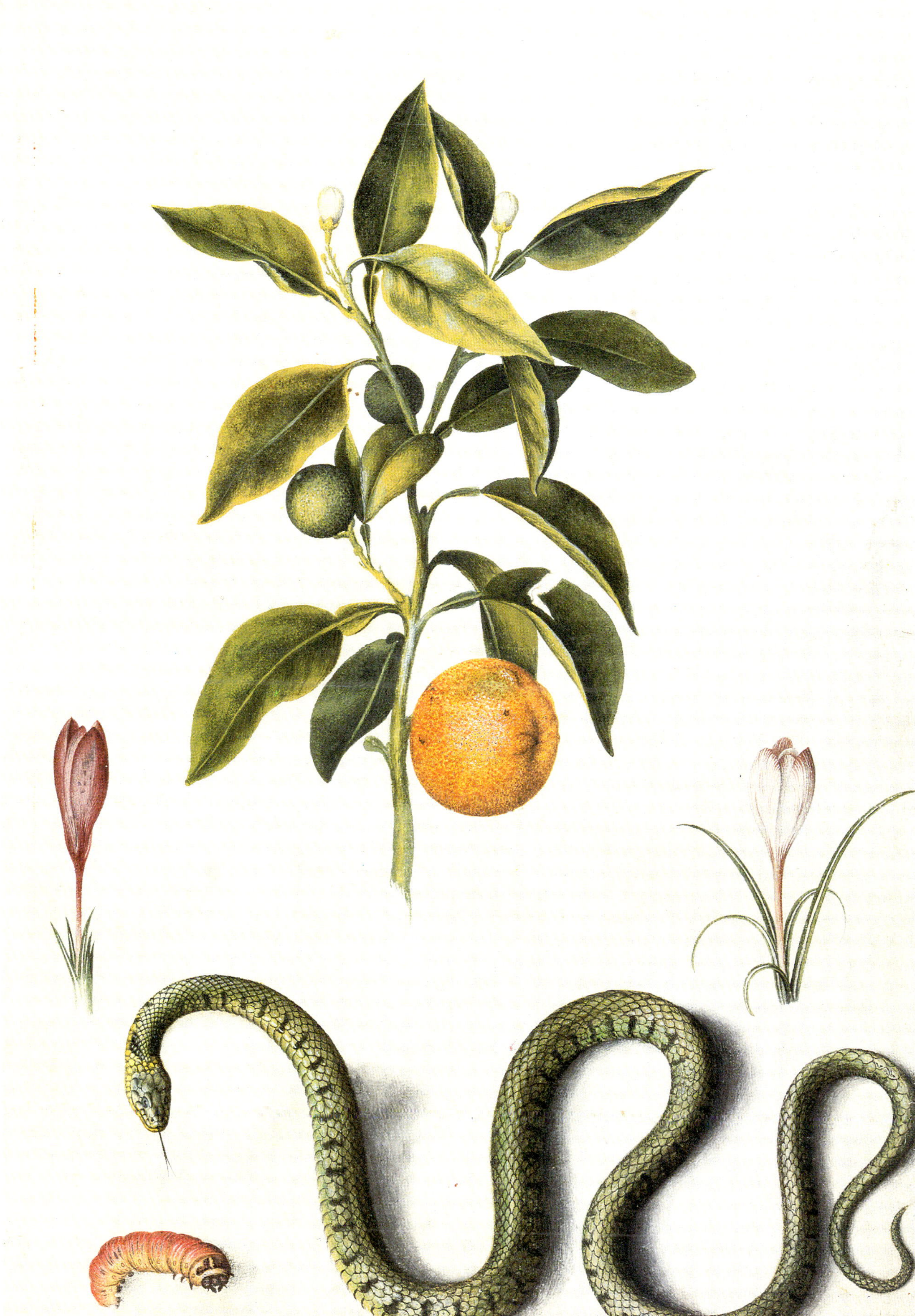

Gentians

Gentian, the small spring
Gentianella verna
Small Gentian of the Spring

Reading the words above, the field botanist at once thinks of the banks and meadows of Upper Teesdale where the Spring Gentian still grows wild. But this is not the rare plant with the sharply pointed blue petals. It is more likely to be the Garden Spring Gentian, *G. acaulis* (though it has rather a long stalk for a flower that is supposed to have none), or *G. angustifolia* or, more probably *G. clusii*. Parkinson's Spring Gentian is also like Marshal's, although he wrote that he had heard that other Spring Gentians were to be found wild in England.

Why our own Spring Gentian survived in just this one small area of Britain is still a mystery. One view is that during the ice ages there were certain geological formations known as nunataks which were not overrun by ice-sheets from the north, and that the gentians survived on these.

A more likely explanation, however, is that at the close of the last ice age, plants that grew in the south migrated northwards as the ice retreated towards the pole, and that the Spring Gentian was one of these. But while this might account for the presence of the gentian in Teesdale, it does not make clear why Teesdale and nowhere else suited the plant. The experts believe that the crucial factor is the type of limestone soil there. In areas where the gentian grows, the soil is chalky, thin and easily washed away, so forest trees which excluded the light could not grow there.

This leaching-out process continues even today. The numerous springs that drain off the moorland into the river Tees spread a coating of chalky soil and boulders over wide areas and so prevent the growth of the sphagnum moss which elsewhere converts large areas of moor into blanket peat bog. Furthermore Teesdale has the cool and moist climate which the gentian favours.

One might wonder, perhaps, why the gentian is not to be seen in the many other mountainous areas of Britain and Scotland where the climate could also be described as cool and moist. But we are told that most of our mountains consist of solid granite – otherwise they would have been broken up long ago by the weather – and that granite is acidic and unfavourable for gentians. But in a very few mountainous areas, some suitable basic strata have been forced up through the granite to the surface. One such locality is the Ben Lawers mountain near Killin, Tayside.

Here a smaller species, the Snow Gentian, growing to only a few inches in height, appears as an annual, but is less easily seen, as its blooms open only in direct sunlight.

The two gentians are shown on the right, opposite

A garden variety of *Gentiana verna*, known as *angulosa* is still a popular rock-garden plant: it has the same bright blue, separated, windmill-sail petals as the Teesdale plant.

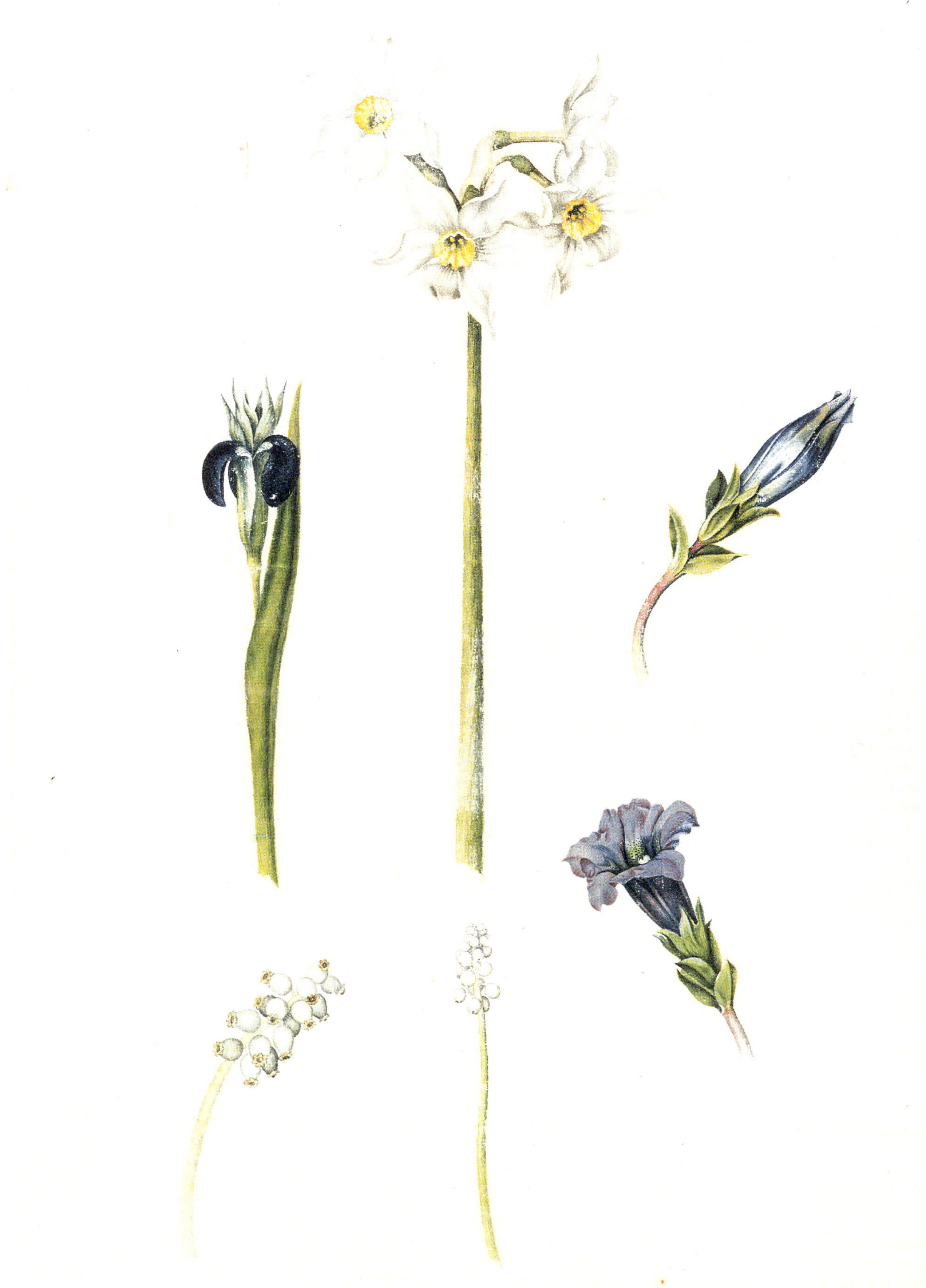

Daffodil & Grape Hyacinths

Daffodil, French early
narssisus narbonensis major ample flore
siue media lutens
The early French dafodill

The early French daffodil with its white petals and yellow corona had long been a feature of English gardens before Marshal painted it. Parkinson in his *Paradisi in Sole* tells us that 'The first of these Daffodils, was brought into England by Mr. Iohn de Franqueuille the elder, who gathered it in his owne Countrey of Cambray, where it groweth wilde, from whose sonne, Mr. Iohn de Franqueuille, now liuing, we all haue had it. The rest have come from Constantinople at severall times; and the last is thought to come from Cyprus. Wee haue it credably affirmed also, that it groweth in Barbary about Fez and Argiers.'

From Parkinson's description it seems that the plant was miserly with its offsets: 'The leauves of this Daffodill, spring vp out of the ground a moneth or two sometimes before the other of this kinde, that follow; being also shorter, and narrower: the stalke likewise is not very high, bearing diuers flowers at the top, breaking through a thinne skinne, as is vsuall with all the Daffodils, euery one whereof is small, consisting of six white leaues, and a small yellow cup in the middle, which is of a prettie small sent, nothing so strong as many others: the roote is great and round, and seldome parteth into of-sets, euen as all the other that follow, bearing many single flowers, doe.'

The Early French Daffodil is shown on p.27, top centre

The 'ache couleur muscaria' and the 'Grape flower, white' which Marshal billed as *hiasintus botroiades flore albo* are considerably less attractive that those we have in gardens today: for example *Muscari moschatum* which ages to an ivory colour only after it has displayed itself for a while in pale mauve.

Parkinson tells us that 'Some English Gentlewomen call the white Grape-flower Pearles of Spaine', and gives us some indications of its origins: 'They grow naturally in many places both of Germany and Hungary; in Spaine likewise, and on Mount Baldus in Italy, and Narbone in France, about the borders of the fields: we haue them in our Gardens for delight.'

Two Grape Hyacinths are shown on the bottom of p.27

An Iris

Iris, velvet
Iris tuberoso
the veluet Iris

'Velvet Floure de-luce hath many long square leaves, spongeous or full of pith, trailing upon the ground, in shape like to the leaves of rushes; among which riseth up a stalk of a foot high bearing at the top a Floure like the Fleure de-luce. The lower leaves that turne downward [i.e. the falls of the flower] are of a perfect blacke colour, soft and smooth as is blacke Velvet; the blacknesse is welted about with greenish yellow, or as wee terme it a Goose-turd greene, of which colour the uppermost leaves [the standards of the flower] do consist.'

John Gerard who provided this sketch realized that this plant with disproportionately large standards and strange root from which fingers projected was no ordinary iris and voted it to be a bastard iris.

Today it is placed in a separate genus and is known as *Hermodactylis* (the fingers of Hermes) *tuberosa*. The plant is also distinctive among irises in that the divisions of the placenta (the part of the ovary to which the ovules are attached) do not meet to divide the ovary into three cells.

At the time of the revised edition of Gerard's *Herbal* (1633), these flowers were not common in England: 'except it be among some few diligent Herbarists in London, who haue them in their gardens, where they increase exceedingly, especially the last described, which is said to grow wilde about Constantinople, Morea, and Greece: from whence it hath been transported into Italy.'

The Iris is shown on p.27, left

Fritillaries

Crown Imperial
Coronna Inperilis
The Croune Imperial

Fritillaries are of two kinds – the demure and the resplendent. The Crown Imperial which we see here rises to the height of 40 inches and is at its best when planted in groups and not left to stand in the manner of a lone pine. The leaves, glossy and bright green, are carried in whorls on the stems, which rise, straight as pikes, to support the ring of bell-like flowers. These can be yellow, orange or red, and are surmounted by a magnificent green top-knot.

The Crown Imperial has been a favourite plant in gardens of the temperate zone for centuries. Some authorities believe it to have originated in the Himalayas and that it was carried thence to Persia as an introduced plant. But few readers will forget the impression made on Vita Sackville-West when, in one of the wildest parts of Persia, in a dark shadowy ravine amid overhanging trees and ferns, she came across a group of Crown Imperials, 'glowing like lanterns in the darkness'. They were growing wild in what she was sure was their native home.

Fritillaria imperialis, to give it its formal name, was known to Charles de l'Ecluse (or Clusius) in Vienna as the Persian Lily, and reached British shores before the end of the sixteenth century, by which time, according to Gerard, there were plenty of them in London gardens. Its pungent smell has been described by Will Ingwersen, the distinguished plantsman, as 'one of those odours which, although immediately repellent, calls back one's nose repeatedly for another exploratory sniff'.

Marshal also painted the pink and white forms of our own native fritillary, *Fritillaria meleagris*, which is now a rare and protected species, though it can occasionally be found in water-meadows and grows to a height of about eighteen inches.

The Latin name for its chequered pink form comes from *fritillus*, a Roman dice-box commonly used with a chequered board, and *meleagris*, that chequer-board apparition, the guinea-fowl. As for the origin of its popular name, Snake's-head: when still in bud, the flower stems not yet upright writhe above the grass, and at the head of each is the head of a snake, poised to strike, narrow, pointed, reptilian and white veined with black. The transformation into a wonderful flower can take as long as three weeks.

The two narcissi illustrated here are said to be '*medio purpureus precox*', that is, early flowering medium-sized purple narcissus, and indeed the corona of both flowers does appear to be dark blue-violet. No specific description is given of the auriculas.

The Fritillary is shown opposite, centre

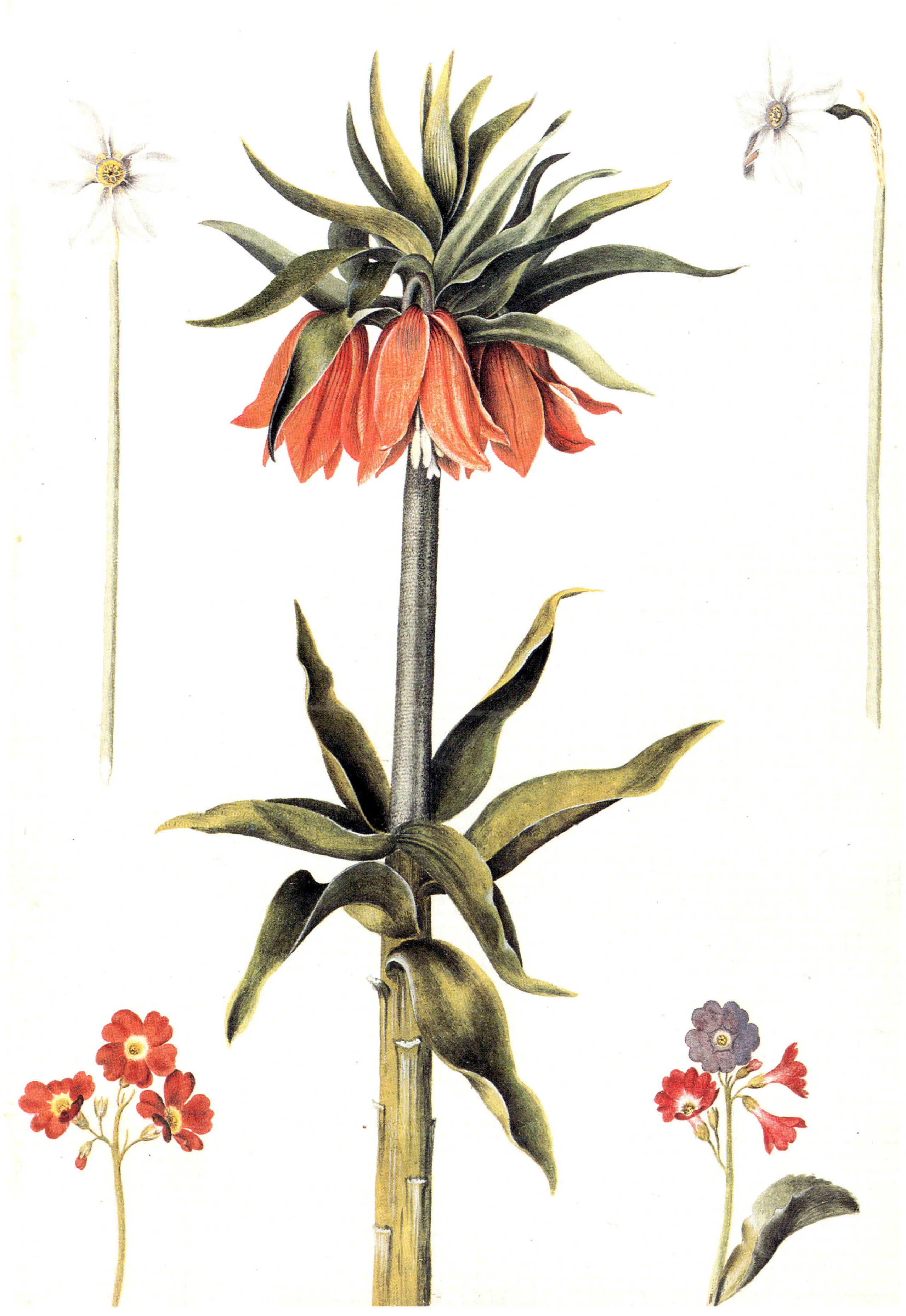

Some Auriculas

Auricula – the double stripe and variegated

Marshal gives us a fine selection of the auriculas available in his day. But they are flowers in transition – and far removed from the heraldic varieties that stare so haughtily at us from the prints of a century or so later. In particular we notice that the eyes in the centre of the flowers are clouded rather than white, the petals are separated and not overlapped in the modern style, and they are notched at the top instead of showing a rounded rim.

The original *Primula auricula*, already beloved in the great days of Rome, still grows on ledges and crannies high up in the Alps, the Apennines and the Carpathian mountains, in places inaccessible to gardeners, leading some of them to call it the Precipice Plant. The flowers are of a brilliant yellow and sweetly scented. The inmost part of the flower, the tube, containing the stamens and pistil, is golden, and the next concentric band, known as the eye, is white, and is surrounded on the outside by the broad yellow band of the body. In the younger plants the leaves are mealy, and covered with a substance often referred to as 'farina', though, in fact, it is composed of minute drops of wax exuded by the individual hairs. The adult leaves are provided with a cartilaginous margin which helps, no doubt, to protect them from the ravages of wind and ice, but they are hairless, and the modern show plant, in which the eye is so thickly dusted that it is referred to as the 'paste', seems to have evolved from a cross between *Primula auricula* and the purple-flowered *Primula hirsuta*, which yielded *Primula × pubescens*.

Clusius noticed the hybrid when he was working in Vienna as gardener in the service of the Emperor Maximilian II and, by 1578, it had reached the Low Countries. The refugee Huguenots who settled in Norwich and Spitalfields and founded the earliest Garden Societies became acknowledged auricula specialists and there were also 'Walloons about London' in Marshal's time who brought plants 'over out of France and Flanders to sell' to nurserymen. The plants were traditionally called Bear's Ear, a name suggested by the shape of the leaves; the synonym '*auricula*' meaning little ear was first recorded, according to *The Oxford English Dictionary* in 1665, but Marshal on other pages of his sketchbook uses '*oriculus*', '*oricula*' and even '*auricula*' as captions for this plant. And he was not the first.

Sir Thomas Hanmer, the royalist, who was allowed to retire during the turmoil of the Civil War to his estate in North Wales, grew forty named sorts of Bear's Ear. Immense pains were taken in Marshal's time and afterwards to bring on the plants and it was recommended that they should be raised in a soil of unusual quality, consisting of goose dung, steeped in bullocks' blood with two parts of baker's sugar scum, two parts of night soil, three parts of yellow loam taken from molehills and a quantity of sea sand.

Inevitably a sharp distinction had to be made – and still exists today – between the Show Auricula with its fine farina so easily spoiled by rain, and the hardy Alpine Auricula of the garden border.

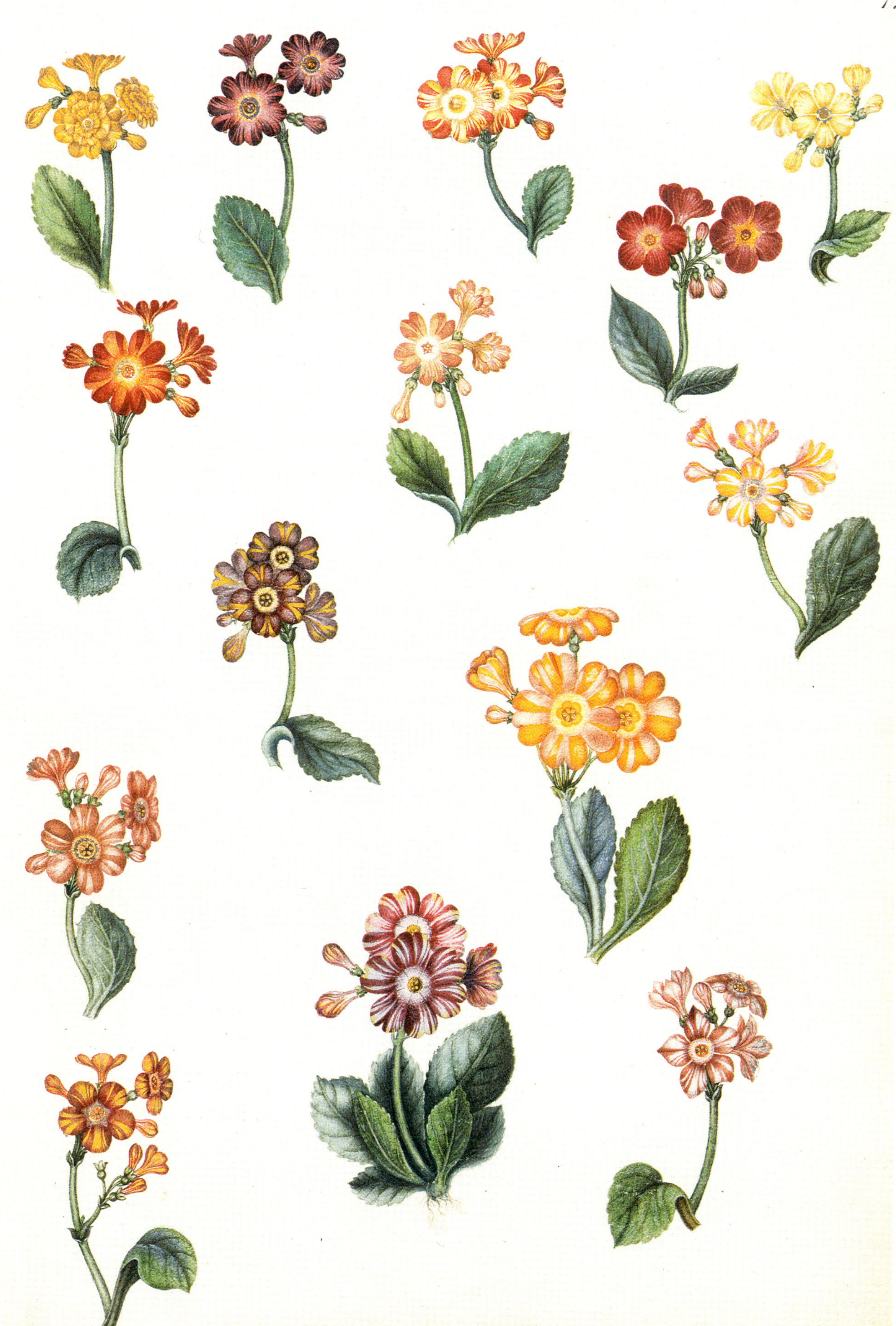
1.

A Yellow Garlic

Molly Broad leaf
Moly Latifolium flore flavo
Broad leaued Moly or Sorcerer garlike with the yelloe flouer

Moly was originally *mûlam,* the Sanskrit word for root. The Greeks, however, used Moly to describe a myth-wreathed magical plant having a black root and a white flower. Homer said that Hermes gave it to Odysseus to help him to resist the spells of Circe. But which plant had Homer really meant?

There was general agreement that it would be one of the Alliums but some of these were more respectable than others. Garlic was accepted in the vegetable garden, John Parkinson remarking that it is 'of a very strong smell and taste, as everyone knoweth, passing either Onions or Leekes, but exceeding wholesome withall for those that can take it'. *Allium ursinum,* Ramsoms, which grows wild in many woods, was also admitted to Parkinson's kitchen garden despite the fact that it had white flowers. If the housewife used the plant in her kitchen it could not have been a spell-binder. Some forms of wild garlic, if closely related to kitchen-garden plants, were not considered to be Molys. Those that were suspect included 'The greatest Moly of Homer' which had whitish flowers dashed over with a wash of purple colour; Dioscorides his Moly; Serpents Moly; and the one we see here which eventually carried off the title *Allium moly,* the Moly of Molys.

Describing this Yellow Moly, Parkinson wrote: 'The yellow Moly hath but one long and broad leafe which it doth not beare flower, but when it will beare flower, it hath two long and broad leaves, yet one alwaies longer and broader than the other, which are both of the same colour, and near the bignesse of a reasonable Tulipa leafe: between the leaves groweth a slender stalke, bearing at the toppe a tuft or umbel of yellow flowers out of a skinnie hose, which parteth three wayes, made of six leaves [petals] a peece, laid open like a Starre, with a greenish backe or outside, and with some yellow threads in the middle . . . the roote is whitish, two for the most part ioyned together, which increaseth quickly, and smelleth very strongly of Garlicke, as both flowers and leaves doe also.'

The Yellow Moly was considered attractive enough for Sir Thomas Hanmer to include it in a garden from which some alliums were omitted as being 'of little beauty'. 'It bears in May,' he said.

Today, despite competition from the giant reddish purple tennis balls of *Allium giganteum* from the Himalayas, and more recently the golf balls of *Allium mirum, Allium moly* under the name of Golden Garlic is a plant which can be naturalized even on clay soil, though, in the wild, it prefers a bed of limestone.

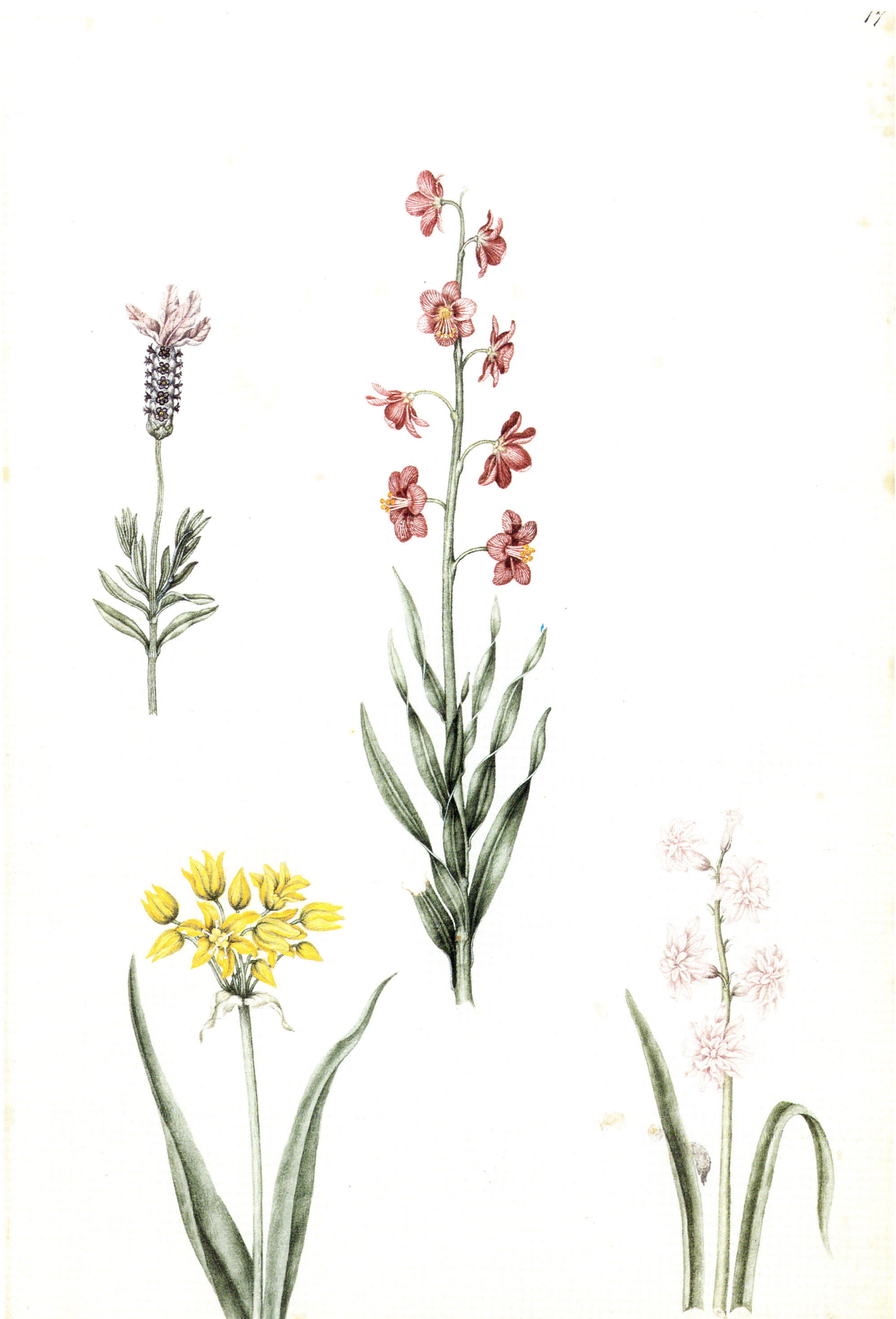
17

A Fritillary

Lilly, Persian
Lilium persicum
The persian Lillie

Parkinson in his *Paradisi in Sole Paradisus Terrestris*, published in 1629, described these flowers as 'smaller than in any other kinde of Lilly, yea not so bigge as the flower of a Fritillaria, consisting of six leaves [petals] a peece, of a dead or overworn purplish colour . . .' and noted that the root was similar to that of the Crown Imperial Fritillary, but 'whiter, rounder, and a little longer, smaller, and not stinking at all like it'.

In comparing it with a fritillary, Parkinson anticipated Linnaeus who named it *Fritillaria persica*. Despite its unscented root, it is not much grown today.

Gerard's comments are worth recording: 'The Persian Lilly hath for his root a great white bulb firme or solid full of juyce, which commonly each yeare setteth off or encreaseth one other bulbe, and sometimes more, which the next yeare after is taken from the mother root, and so bringeth forth such floures as the old plant did. From this root riseth up a fat thicke and straight stemme of two cubits high, whereupon is placed long narrow leaues of a greene colour, declining to blewnes as doth those of the woade. The floures grow alongst the naked part of the stalke like little bels, and an ouer-worne purple colour, hanging down their heads, euery one hauing his owne foot-stalke of two inches long, as also his pestell or clapper from the middle part of the floure; which being past and withered, there is not found any seed at all, as in other plants, but is increased onely in his root.

'The Persian Lilly groweth naturally in Persia and those places adiacent, whereof it tooke his name, and is now (by the industrie of Trauellers into those countries, louers of Plants) made a Denizon in some few of our London gardens.

'This Persian Lilly is called in Latine, *Lilium Persicum, Lilium Susianum, Pennacio Persiano*, and *Pannaco Persiano*, either by the Turks themselues, or by such as out of those parts brought them into England; but which of both is vncertaine. *Alphonsus Pancius*, Physition to the Duke of Ferrara, when as he sent the figure of this Plant vnto *Carolus Clusius*, added this title, *Pennacio Persiano è Pianta bellissima & è specie di Giglio ó Martagon, diuerso della corona Imperiale*: This is in English, This most elegant plant *Pennacio* of Persia is a kind of Lilly or Martagon, differing from the floure called the Crowne Imperiall.'

A Fritillary is shown on p.35, centre

Tufted Lavender

Sage, wild of Arabia
Steachus Arabicum'
steacus of Arabia

This is a portrait of *Lavandula stoechas*, French Lavender, complete with its top-knot of purple bracts which give colour to the spikes long after the flowers are over. The plant was known to be especially abundant on the Staechades Islands 'which are over against Marselles' and which we know as the Iles d'Hyères. In Marshal's time it was sometimes known as Sticadove, a corruption of Staechades, and, as far back as 1578 as Cassidony. The derivation of this word is unknown, unless we take a chance and assume that it might be a corruption of Chalcedony.

Gerard wrote: 'These herbes do grow wilde in Spaine, in Languedocke in France, and in the Islands called Stoechades ouer against Massilia: we haue them in our gardens, and keepe them with great diligence from the iniurie of our cold clymate. . . . They are sowne of seed in the end of April, and couered in the Winter from the cold, or els set in pots or tubs with earth, and carried into houses . . . .

'The Apothecaries call the floure *Staecados*: in English, French Lauander, Steckado, Stickadoue, Cassidonie, and some simple people imitating the same name do call it *Cast me Downe* . . . .

'French Lauender saith *Galen* is of temperature compounded of a little cold earthie substance, by reason whereof it bindeth: it is of force to take away obstructions, to extenuate or make thinne, to scoure and clense, and to strengthen not onely all the entrails, but the whole bodie also . . . .

'*Dioscorides* teacheth that the decoction hereof doth helpe the diseases of the chest, and is with good successe mixed with counterpoisons.

'The later Physitions affirme, that *Staechas*, and especially the floures of it, are most effectuall against paines of the head, and all diseases thereof proceeding of cold causes, and therefore they be mixed in all compositions almost which are made against head-ache of long continuance, the Apoplexie, and the falling sicknesse, and such like diseases.

'The decoction of husks and floures drunke, openeth the stoppings of the liuer, the lungs, the milt, the mother, the bladder, and in one word all other inward parts, clensing and driuing forth all euill and corrupt humours, and procuring urine.'

The French do not think highly of *La Lavande Staechade*, which they more often call *Lavande à toupet*. They say it will grow only at low altitudes, where land is expensive, and that it is not worth gathering for perfume. It is none too hardy in British gardens either.

Tufted Lavender is shown on p.35, top left

The flower on the right of the plate is described as the Double Oriental Hyacinth.

The Violet and a Zumbul

Violet, blue single
viola simplex martia
Single March violet

For a small plant with a small flower, the violet has received a disproportionately large amount of attention. The Athenians adopted it as their symbol or logo. It was special to Aphrodite. Pliny praised it, and Virgil, in mourning for Daphne, deplored the fact that there were no violets on her coffin. The Romans used it in a scented paste applied to their room-walls, and greeted their guests with a violet-scented cloud of vapour dispensed from the wings of tame doves.

Like many orchids, the violet presents a flower that is 'upside down', that is, one that has turned through a half-circle of 180 degrees before opening, so that the petal to which the nectar spur is attached takes up the lowest position. The flowers that open are pollinated by bees but the plant's reputation for modesty is sustained by the fact that some of the flowers can pollinate themselves without ever opening.

The scent of the Sweet Violet, the only British wild species to have any, contains a compound known as Ionone, a methyl ketone which has a soporific effect on the sense of smell, so that, after a few sniffs, the scent appears to vanish, only to return again after the sniffer has recovered his breath.

The Parma Violet, promoted by ex-Empress Marie Louise after her retirement to her estates in that part of Italy, was regarded in the nineteenth century as the most finely scented variety and until the 1900s was the main variety grown commercially in the south of France. But though its double flowers were magnificent, the plant proved to be tender, and furthermore needed four years to reach maturity. Today, the Victoria Violet, a single-petalled variety, has replaced the Parma in Tourettes-sur-Loup and other villages near Grasse where violet cultivation still provides a livelihood. The flowers have a richer, darker colour than the Parma, are more resistant to disease, and they take but two years to develop.

Already in the nineteenth century the cost of picking the individual flowers to be used for scent was high, and the outlay today would be prohibitive. Instead, the earliest blooms are air-lifted to the florists' showrooms, and when premium prices are no longer obtainable the remaining flowers are diverted to the confectionery trade to decorate chocolates as crystallised violets.

The leaves are harvested separately and yield an odour which, though pleasantly 'green' to the senses, is compatible with the flowers, or, rather, with the synthetics which are mainly used as a replacement.

But even the leaves are not a high-yield source, and by the time they have been subject to distillation and filtration processes, the cost of the violet 'absolute' (to use the perfumery trade term) currently works out at between £3,000 and £4,000 per kilogramme.

The hyacinth in the centre of the page is *Hyacinthus indicus orientalis* – 'the Great oriental Jacinth or Zumbul'. The anemones at the head and foot of this page are unnamed.

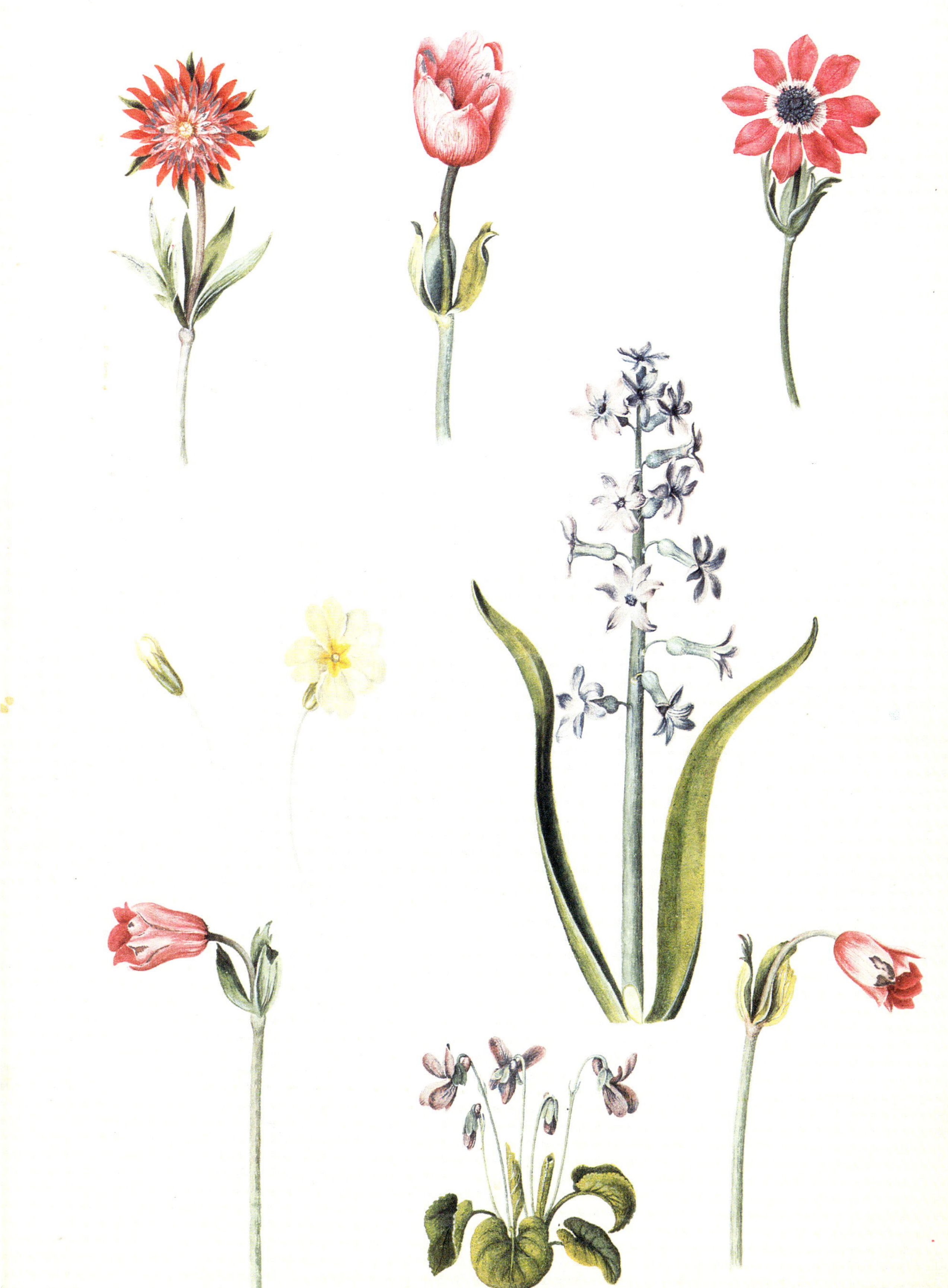

The Dog's Tooth Violet and Two Narcissus

Dog's teeth, red, 3
Dents Canninus flore rubro
dogs teeth with a read flouer

The Dog's Tooth Violet is actually a member of the lily tribe. *Erythronium dens canis*, being a lily, springs from a bulb, and it has been suggested that 'Dog's teeth' describes the offsets from the bulb which are sharply pointed, but it might also refer to the flower petals which are reflexed upwards in the manner of a cyclamen.

This is one of the exotics which did not need to cross the Atlantic to reach Britain. Gerard declared that it grew in 'Germanie, Italie, in Styria not far from Gratz, as also Modena and Bononia in Italie'.

It is a dainty plant, a mere six inches in height with mottled leaves. Marshal painted the red variety, but today the colour more often seen is pinkish mauve or 'delayed purple' as Parkinson put it. Since his day other varieties have come to decorate the flower-bed, including the mottled American Trout Lily, and the yellow-flowered varieties from California.

Three examples of the Dog's Tooth Violet are shown at the bottom of the page opposite

On the same page Marshal has included the Striped Anemone, the Fine-leaved Full-Flowered Crimson Anemone, and the Fine-leaved Peach-coloured Anemone. A wide variety of other anemones is to be seen on nearby pages. These would be only a small selection of what he could have seen in Sir Thomas Hanmer's garden where there were scarlets, straw-coloured flowers, dove-coloured, white and 'gridelines' (literally flax-grey but used more often to denote greyish mauve or even purple). Some were striped and some bordered with contrasting edging. Most of them would have been derived from *Anemone coronaria* which has yielded the two most popular strains of today: the single 'de Caen' variety and the double or semi-double St Brigid. No clear blue garden anemone had been developed at that time like the wild one in the picture.

Daffodil, Spanish small
pseudonarcissus hispanicus minor bastard
the small daffodil of Spaine

Daffodill non Pariel White
dafedill nonparille nurcitus tottus albus monta[na]
Sive nonpariele amplo Ca[lice]

Marshal managed to fit in two daffodils on this page.

Parkinson knew the White Narcissus illustrated here. To him it was '*Narcissus montanus sive Nompareille totus albus amplo calice*'. The '*amplo calice*' or 'cup', to use Parkinson's word, referred to what we call the trumpet or corona which gives protection to the stamens of the flower.

The small daffodil looks something like Wordsworth's but the trumpet of our wild daffodil is scarcely expanded at the mouth.

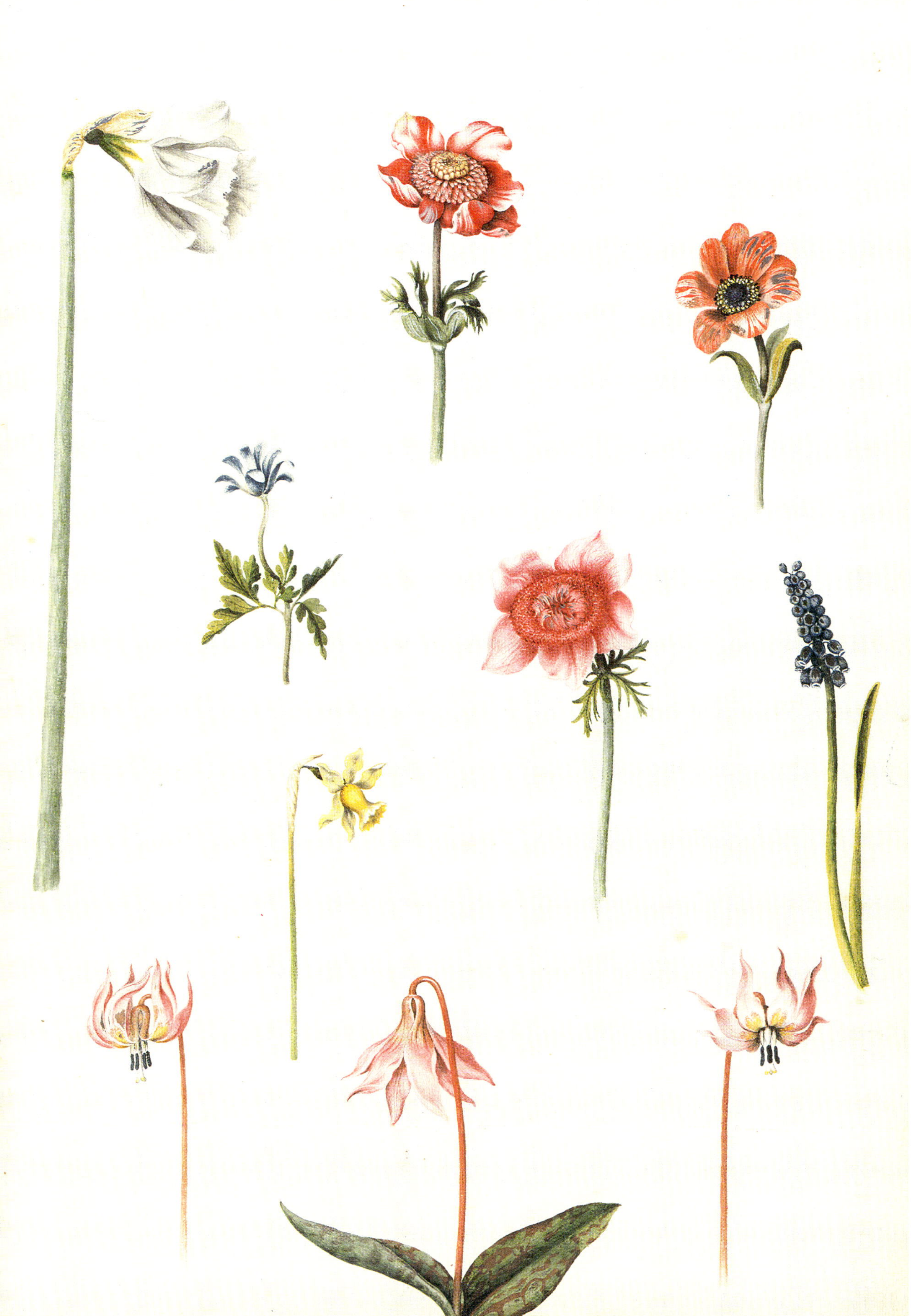

Green-Winged Orchid

Satirion Royal of Naples, female
Palma Christi foemina
The female Satirion Royall

Palma Christi, the palm or hand of Christ, originally referred to the Castor-oil Plant, *Ricinus communis*, the leaves of which were shaped like a hand. Later, however, the description was also applied to the roots of certain orchids, the tubers of which looked like fingers. In Britain these are classified under the heading of *Dactylorhiza* meaning 'finger-rooted', and this sector includes both Spotted and Marsh Orchids that still grow wild where they can.

The Green-Winged Orchid is shown bottom centre opposite

The orchid shown here is *Orchis morio*, the Green-winged Orchid, the flowers of which are easily distinguishable by their purple helmets striped with dark-green lines. The plant's roots, however, are not palmate, but round and bulbous, so the name Satirion, or perhaps Satyrion, associated with those orchids having testicular roots, would be more appropriate. But, in that case, the flower would need to be masculine and not feminine.

The orchid shown on the bottom left of the page in Marshal's sketchbook and called the 'male Satirion Royall' is *Orchis praetermissa*, the Southern Marsh Orchid, which has unspotted leaves, though it is much larger than the Green-winged Orchid.

Marshal, of course, would not have sent to Naples for the Green-winged Orchid. It is a native plant of the meadows particularly in pastures which have not been 'improved' or ploughed. It has become less widespread over the years, and some of its best sites now lie within the safety of country churchyards.

Marshal elsewhere shows (on folio 68 – not illustrated here) the 'bee flower orchis' for which he gives the Latin name *testiculus vulpinus sphegodes*. This accords with 'Fox-stones' which was one of the many popular names for it. *Sphegodes* has since been allotted to the Early Spider Orchid, which has green sepals, clearly distinguishable from the pink sepals of the Bee Orchid.

At the head of this page we see a fine-leaved, regularly marked flower described as 'anemone amarantie' an adjective which, in its original form, denoted a fabulous flower that never faded. The hyacinth in the centre is said to be 'the common oriental jacinth'.

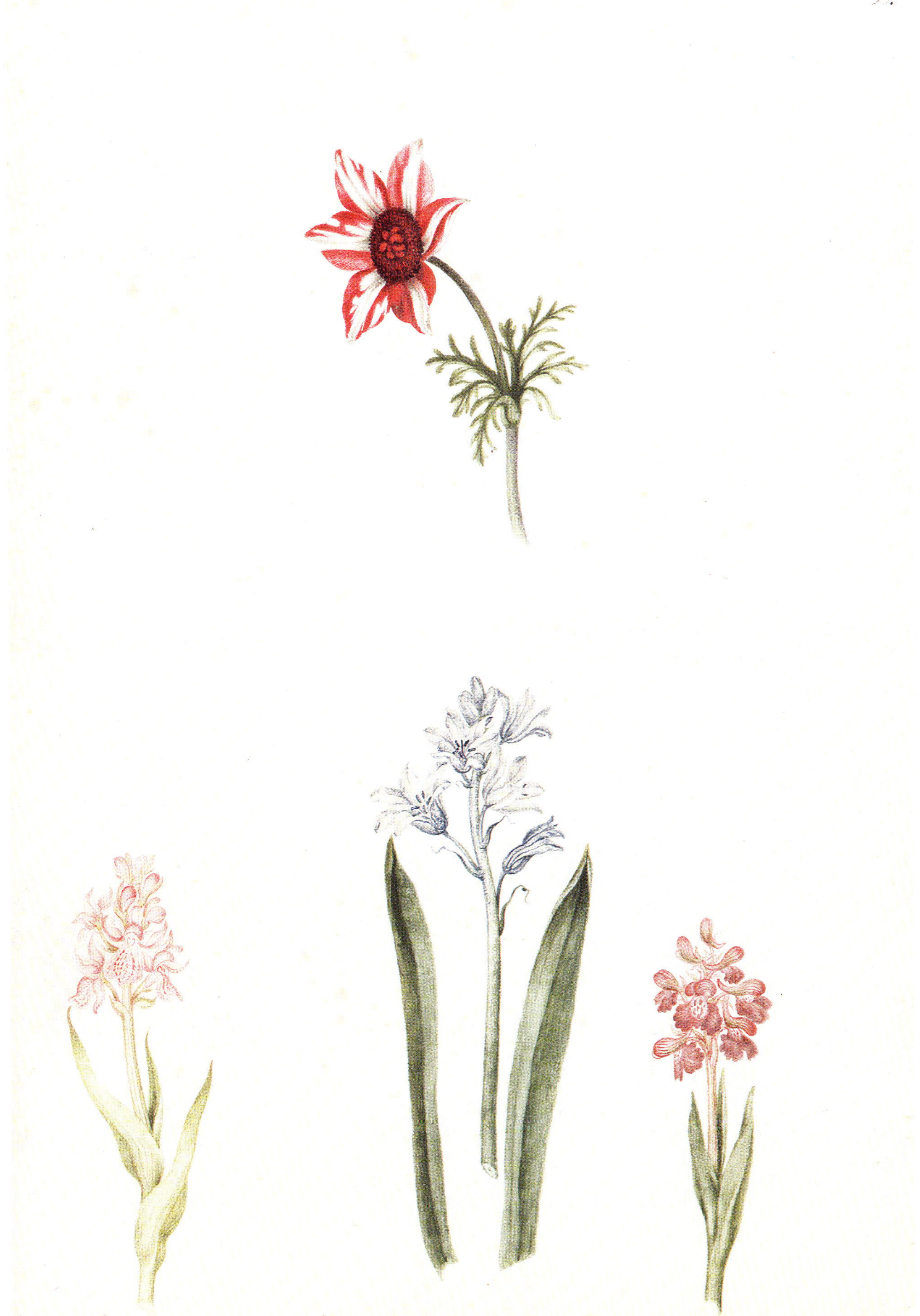

21.

The Pansy

Violet
Viola flamea sive tricolor flos trinitates pense
Pense

Marshal called his plant 'pense' – his rendering of its French name '*pensé*'. Here is a member of the violet family, with one of its flowers which has been born upside down. Pansy experts declare that it seldom occurs with modern hybrids, but we can be sure that an artist of Marshal's integrity would not have drawn this portrait from hearsay.

Known as the *Viola flamea* because of the flower's lively orange centre, it was also called the Trinity Flower because of its three colours: white, purple and yellow. To Parkinson it was the Ordinary Garden Pansy or Heartsease, and he showed no special enthusiasm for it, classing it as a violet with a variety of dainty colours but no scent. He found these plants to be 'so variably mixed with blew or purple, white or yellow, that it is hard to set down all the varieties'. But here there was variety in a single plant, with blotches on the lower petals of all three flowers, but not on all the upper petals.

In 1839 the first centrally blotched pansy appeared. It was a casual that had seeded itself among some heathers in Lord Gambier's garden at Iver in Buckinghamshire, and was noticed and picked out by his gardener, William Thompson. Soon the connoisseurs were insisting on having pansies with a large black blotch. Plantsmen started to improve the pansy by hybridizing and selecting the plants showing flowers with colours that were deeper and more formally arranged and with petals the edges of which ran together to make an unbroken circle. Most of the modern hybrids are crosses between the plant that Marshal painted and a garden hybrid *Viola* × *wittrockiana*.

Eventually nurserymen succeeded in breeding a distinctly different 'pansy' by crossing their plants with the Sweet Violet, and the Horned Violet, *Viola cornuta*, which grows a foot high in its native Pyrenees. The result was a plant yielding flowers of many different colours: self, striped, mottled, suffused or margined. But one feature they must not have are the blotches and rays that give so much attraction to the conventional pansy and to Marshal's plant. It seems unfortunate then, that the unblotched newcomers should have appropriated for themselves the 'English' name viola which belongs in Latin to the family as a whole.

The plant on the centre right of the plate is described as the 'Great Latte bulbous flowering violett'. Today we know it as the Summer Snowflake or Loddon Lily after that tributary of the Thames which is one of its haunts. But the modern Latin name still follows the old inaccurate tradition. For *Leucojum aestivum*, translated literally, means 'Summer White Violet'.

The double anemone shown here is described as one of the broad-leaved type.

The cerise striped tulip was already well-established in Marshal's time. These three specimens are credited collectively to 'The Widow Lancsel'.

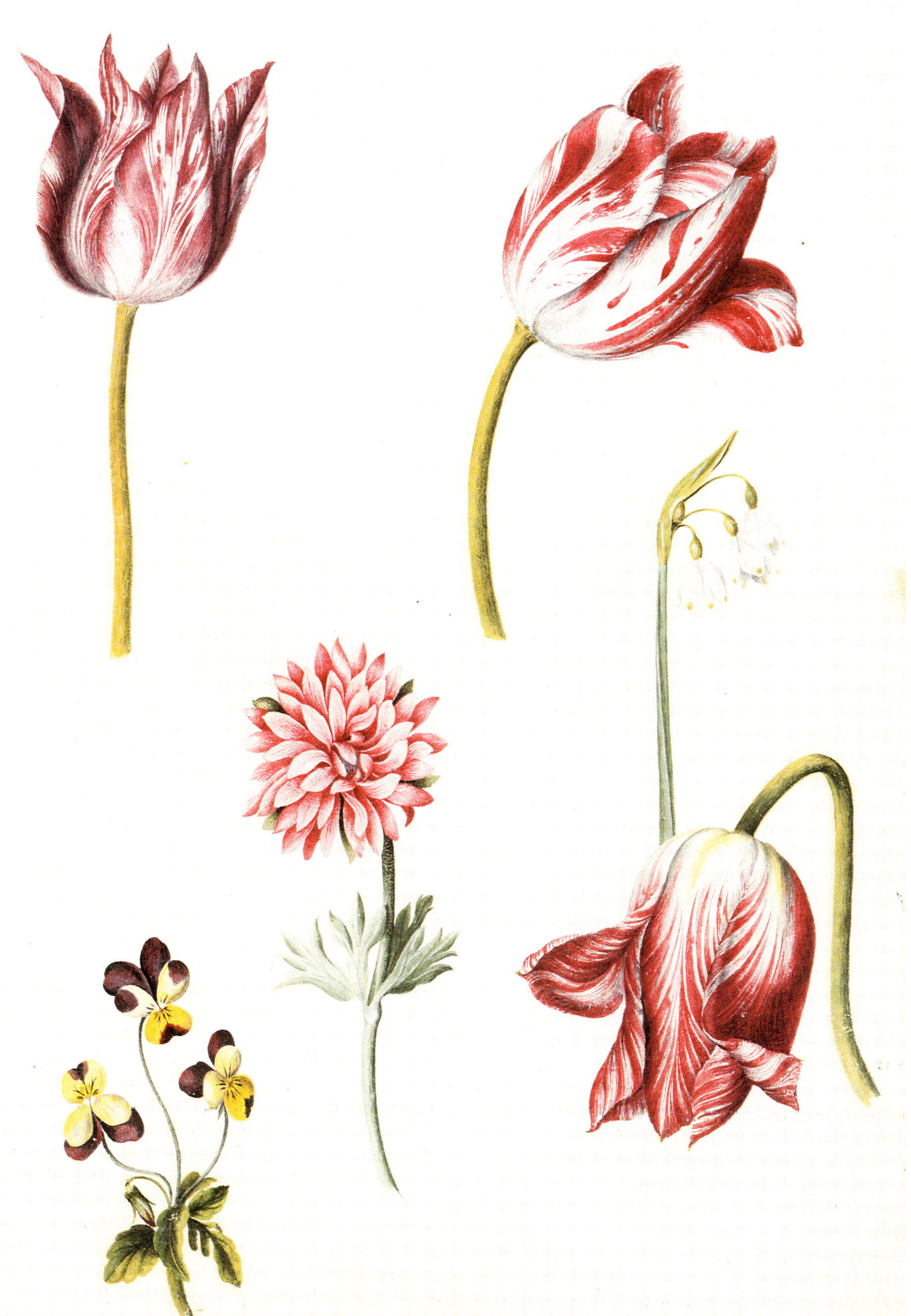

Yellow Horned-Poppy

Poppy, yellow
papaver flore luteo
yealeo popie

This is one of the few seaside flowers to appear in Marshal's sketchbook. The leaves are deeply cut with the lobes pointing hither and thither, giving the plant a confused appearance. The foliage is the colour of green sea-water.

The stout-stemmed Sea Poppy *Glaucium flavum*, which can grow to a height of nearly three feet, is anchored by a tap-root boring deeply into the shingly, wind-swept banks.

The capsule containing the seeds is its most noticeable feature, resembling an outsize French Bean, up to twelve inches long, hairless but rough. This splits into two, uncovering the seeds. As Marshal shows, the two sepals which protected the flower in its bud stage have fallen away (as is the case with the whole poppy family). When in bloom they make a telling contrast against the brilliant blue Viper's Bugloss and pink Sea Rocket, also known in Marshal's day as Red Bunny.

The plant has a long flowering season, too, lasting from June to September, and from the artist's point of view is a most satisfactory plant since it will simultaneously show its pointed green buds, flowers in profusion, and long seed pods.

The Yellow Horned-Poppy is now far less common than in Marshal's day, and has since disappeared from many localities where it was formerly known – such as the north-east coasts of England and Scotland, and the Shetland Isles – and will not grow naturally inland in Britain as it does on the continent of Europe. Nevertheless it can be cultivated as a garden annual from seed sown in March or April on the site where it is to flower. Some gardeners prefer to treat it as a biennial, sowing the seeds nearer to the time when they would have been scattered by the wild plant. The seedlings then are brought on in a cold frame and planted out in October in the bed where they are to flower the following season.

Culpeper mentions this plant and describes it accurately, but he may not have seen it *in situ*. He tells us that it grows among waste grounds, rubbish, and upon walls and buildings – which makes his recommendation to use it as a cure for jaundice and scurvy something less than convincing.

The bloom at the top of the page is described in the Index as 'Tulip, Sloe colour' and by Marshal as 'Prunelle' – another instance of the French connection.

The honeysuckle on the left was named *periclimenum perfoliatum siue Italicum* (Perfoliate or Italian Honeysuckle) in the album, with the French equivalent 'Chevre fieulle' (more properly *Chevrefeuille*) added gratuitously beneath.

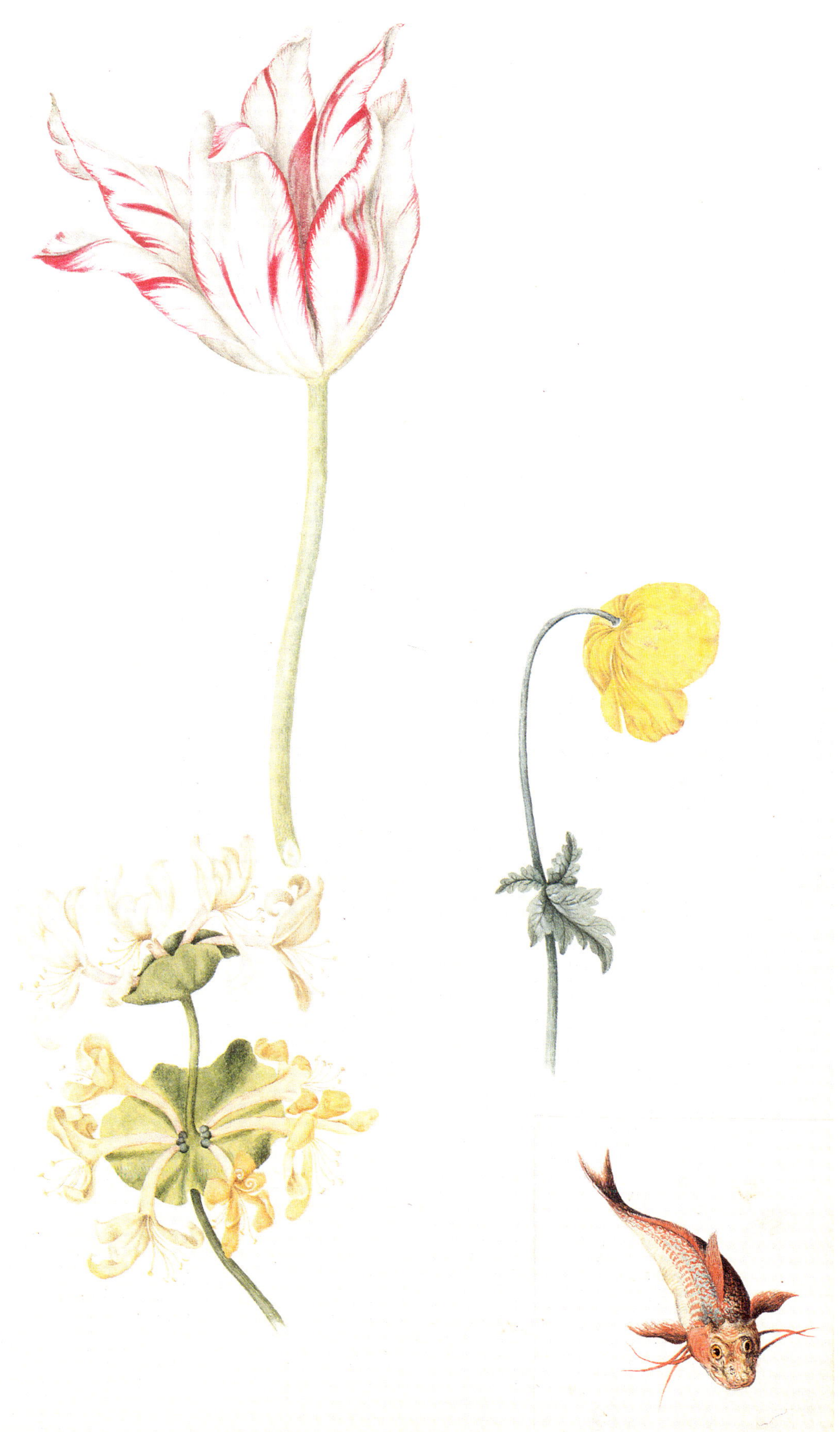

Tulips

Agatte Robin
penelope
yeleo croune

Though several species of tulip grow wild in southern France and northern Italy, and one even in England, the gardeners of Europe took no notice of the plant until 1554 when Ogier Ghiselin de Busbecq, the ambassador representing the Holy See at the Court of the Sultan, noticed the success which the Turks enjoyed with some of the Asiatic species. The ambassador originally saw tulips growing wild in the fields while on a journey from Adrianople to Constantinople, but it was a garden variety that he brought back with him to Vienna. Konrad Gesner, botanist and Alp-mountaineer, saw some growing in Augsburg in 1559 – fragrant and each with a single large red flower, like a lily – and with a sweet scent. He published his description together with the first illustration in 1561.

It was not until 1614 that the first illustration of a striped or 'broken' tulip was published – in the *Hortus Floridus* by Crispin de Passe the younger, a member of the well-established family of Dutch engravers. There followed an incubation period leading up to the years of 'Tulipomania' in the 1630s, during which single bulbs changed hands at amounts equivalent today to more than £2,000.

England, where tulips had first arrived around 1578, was not immune from the fever, and John Parkinson in his *Paradisi in Sole, Paradisus Terrestris* mentions 140 different kinds, including 'A Tulipa of three colours', 'The Tulipa of Caffa purple with pale white stripes', a 'Crimson with White Flames', 'A kind of Zwisser called Goliah', and 'the feathered tulipa, red and yellow'.

Thus a distinction was already being made between tulips that were feathered, that is with the colour confined to the edges of the petals, and those that were flamed, in which colour runs up the centre of each petal, branching out to the edges.

Parrot tulips – broken tulips with petals edged irregularly – came into cultivation soon after the Restoration, and Marshal's tulips faintly suggest the coming trend.

The explanation of why a tulip that is self-coloured, i.e. uniform, unexpectedly 'breaks' into other combinations was not forthcoming until the 1920s, when it was discovered that the colour changes were caused by the attacks of a virus.

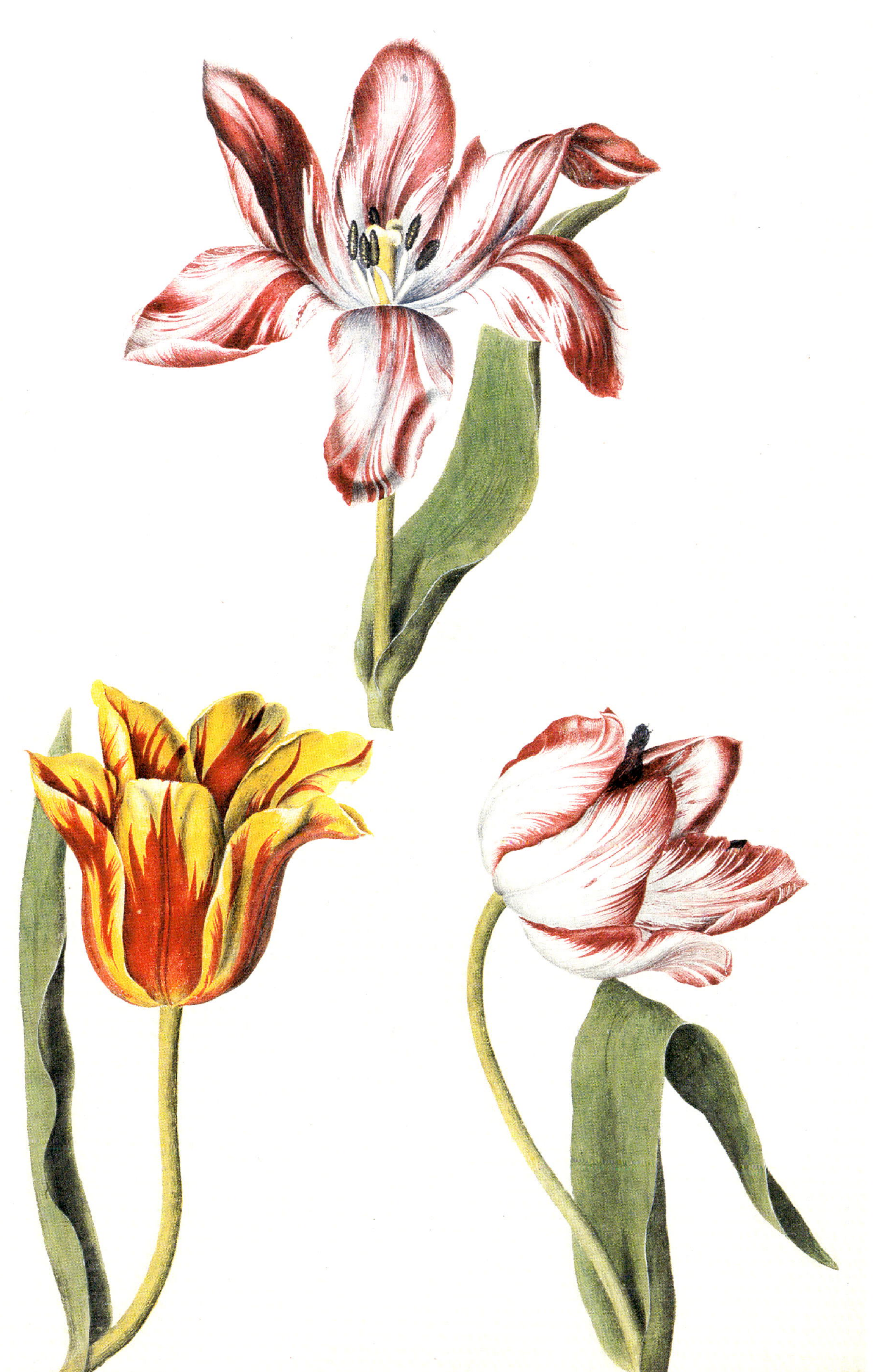

Cranesbills

Crane bill spotted
Ger. Fuscum sive maculatum
Swart tawny or spotted Crane bill

When Walter Fitch, probably the most successful and undoubtedly the most prolific botanical artist of the nineteenth century, wrote a number of articles for *The Gardeners' Chronicle* of 1869 (reproduced in Wilfrid Blunt's delightful book, *The Art of Botanical Illustration*), he paid special attention to the problems of drawing leaves in perspective: 'Leaves have been subjected to more bad treatment by the draughtsman than perhaps any other portion of the vegetable kingdom; they have been represented, or rather misrepresented, in all kinds of impossible positions. Numerous are the tortures to which they have been subjected: dislocated or broken ribs, curious twists, painful to behold – even their wretched veins have not escaped. . . . Here may I impress on the reader, the importance of noting the angle formed by the veins with the midrib, their respective differences apart, their faintness or prominence.'

It is therefore all the more creditable to Marshal that the leaves of *Geranium phaeum*, the Dusky Cranesbill (Marshal preferred the adjective swart i.e. swarthy), should form such a strongly marked feature of this portrait. The irregularly slashed leaves with jagged fjords between the lobes are in sharp contrast to the simply structured prim, demure flowers, with their subfusc petals held wide open – even reflexed. The spots to which Marshal refers are to be seen not on the petals but in the sinuses between the lobes, and are blotches or streaks rather than spots – a reason, perhaps, why this synonym has fallen into disuse.

Something about the Cranesbill family must have appealed to Marshal. It may have been the flowers themselves or the sequel that follows the flowering period, when the seed capsules burst and roll upwards like the strands of a maypole towards the tip of the style to which they are attached. Or it may have been the fact that in those times, when the division between wild and garden flowers was not so rigid, they were more often to be seen in flowerbeds.

'Most of the Cranes bils are strangers unto us by nature but endenizond in our English Gardens,' Parkinson wrote. 'It has been reported unto mee by some of good credit, that the second, or Crowfoot Cranes bill, hath been found naturally growing in England, but yet I never saw it, although I have seen many sortes of wilde kindes in many places.' The Crowfoot Cranesbill so-called from the shape of the leaves which resemble those of the buttercup is clearly the Meadow Cranesbill – *Geranium pratense* – a native plant with flowers of the 'faire blew or watchet colour' specified by Parkinson. It favours positions by the hedgerows and roadsides so it is not surprising that some of Parkinson's acquaintances should have reported it to him.

The *Geranium variegato* (now *Geranium versicolor*, the Streaked Cranesbill) was also in gardens and was painted by Marshal in his sketchbook. Parkinson noted that it was 'so thickly and variably striped with fine small reddish veines, that no green leafe that is of the bignesse can show so many veins in it, nor so thick running as every leafe [petal] of this flower doth'.

Marshal also painted a delightful and delicate portrait of the finely leaved Common Storksbill, *Erodium cicutarium*, which he called without disparagement the Unsavery field Cranebill, to distinguish it from its more coarsely leaved, strong-smelling cousin, the Musky Storksbill.

The Cranesbill is shown centre right opposite

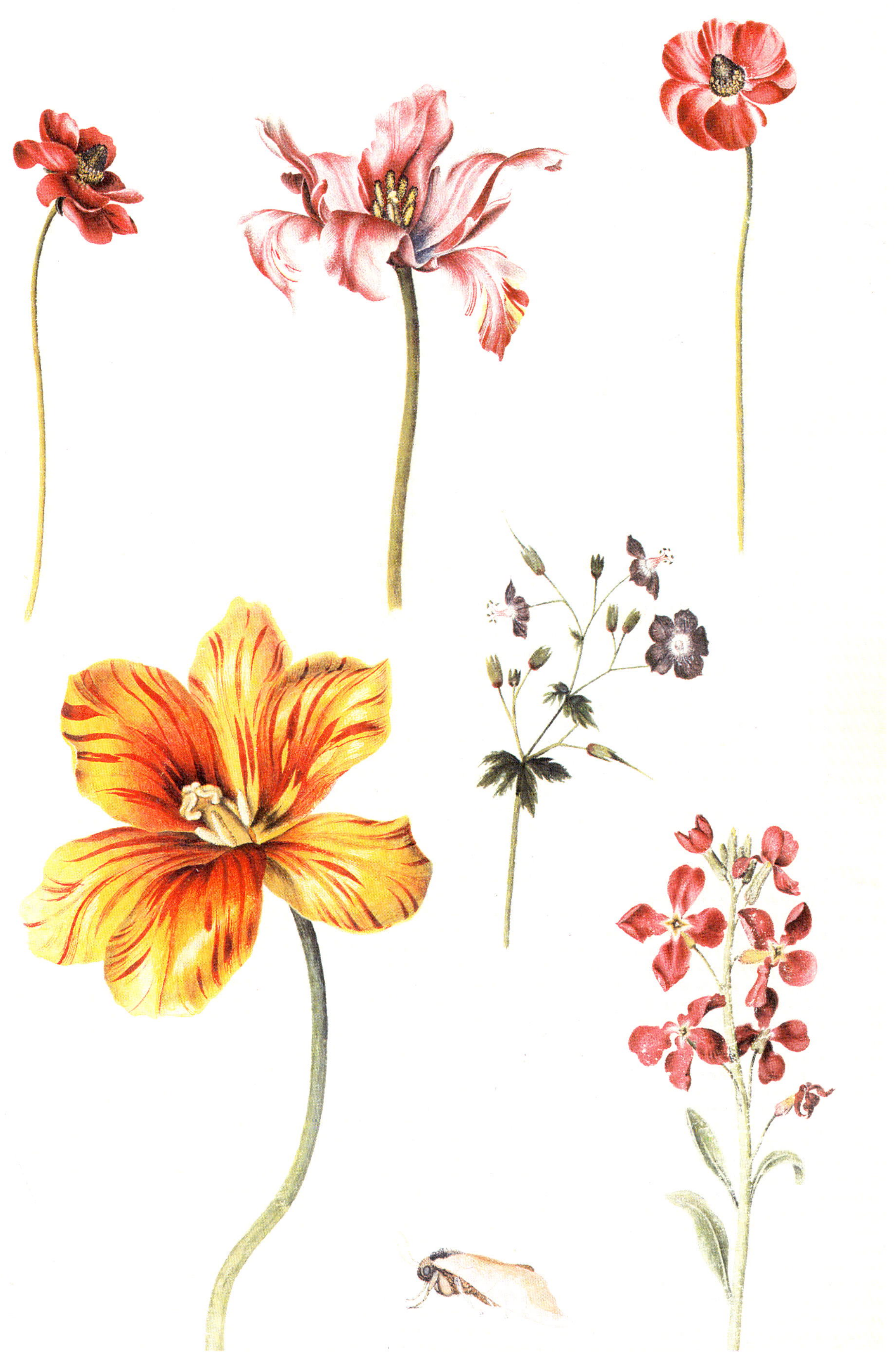

A Miscellany

At the head of this page we see two ranunculus, described as the 'read crowfoot of Asia'. The tulip at the top is described as 'Agett and Sagget' – the stripes being like those of an agate, and the texture, perhaps, like that of *sagatis*, the French word for a lightweight silklike material. The orange tulip variety is named 'Chamelottee', the early form of camlet, which denoted a costly Eastern fabric made of wool, silk, hair or linen. The original Arab word described the pile in velvet, but was later applied to materials made from camel-hair. Plantsmen, even in those days, went to remote lengths in search of a suitable simile for their latest cultivar.

At the lower right hand corner of the page, we see a wild stock ('stoke Juliflower'), such as grows on the cliffs at Rottingdean fairly safely out of reach of plant-lovers.

The Miscellany is shown on p.51

At the foot of the picture is a Poplar Hawkmoth.

Lady's Slipper

Ladies Slipper
Calciolus maria
the Lady Slipper

Here Marshal has provided a worthy portrait of a flower probably grown indoors or under specially favourable conditions because it is considerably larger than our native blooms.

The image of a lady's slipper seems to have occurred to admirers in several parts of Europe. The French named the flower '*Sabot de Vénus*', and the Germans '*Frauenschuh*', and the use of the word '*maria*'* in the Latin name suggests that a more literal translation into English would have been not the Lady's Slipper but Our Lady's Slipper.

Perhaps it was the strongly Lutheran tradition in Sweden that led Linnaeus to make a change, and he finally settled on the name in use today, *Cypripedium calceolus*. Kypris was one of the Greek names for Venus and *pedium* was the Latinized form of the Greek *podion*, a little foot. *Calceolus* is Latin for a small shoe. Orchid-lovers have now elevated the *Cypripediums* to the status of a botanical tribe by virtue of the fact that two anthers are discernible at the top of the column into which the male and female elements of the flower are fused. In other orchids one, or in some species three, can be distinguished.

The *Cypripediums* are unusual in other ways, too. Like other orchids they have six petals, arranged in two whorls. The middle posterior of these petals has been modified to form the 'shoe'; three others at the top and sides of the flower are easily distinguishable, and the remaining two petals are joined together to form a single petal pointing downwards. In some specimens the two points of these joined petals remain separated as in a forked tongue. But in other specimens their individuality has been lost.

In Britain the wild *Cypripedium* has had a romantic if chequered history. When Frederic Arnold Lees wrote his work *The Flora of West Yorkshire*, published in 1888, he recalled that Parkinson in 1640 had given the first record of the plant growing in the West Riding: 'in a wood called the Helkes . . . neere the border of Yorkshire'. (Gerard had described the plant but said only that it was reported to grow 'in the North parts of this Kingdome'.) It was still growing there years later when Ray found it '*In sylva quadam prope montem Ingleborough Helks Wood dicta*'. It disappeared from there many years ago, as deplored by Reginald Farrer, the great botanical explorer who lived nearby. But in a later work written in 1916 Lees gave indications that the orchid was still not impossible to find.

Thus he refers to 'many of both old and young residents having made acquaintance with it upon its erratic flowerings in this or that disturbed or slipped earth nook of scrub wood during the last fifty years!' He goes on to say that its latest discovery in 1906 was made 'by the late Missie Madge Caradice when quite a girl, on a talus bank near Kettlewell, where it is still; not blooming every year but some seasons as in 1909 the clump or colony in the one spot perfected six flower spikes. It has also occurred within memory at Heseltine Gill, under the shadow of Penyghent, in Knipe Wood, in Belmont and in the Sleets Gill Scrub of Lower Arndale.'

It must be said, however, that local botanists working in line abreast a few feet apart have more recently scoured these and other likely sites without known success, and, within the whole region in which the plant was formerly known, that is Yorkshire, Lancashire and Durham, only one plant, or perhaps we should say root system because the spikes come up in a slightly different place from year to year, still survives.

Lady's Slipper is shown on p.55, bottom centre

* It should have been 'Mariae'.

The rhizomes of Lady's Slipper, to quote Dr Lees again, 'are far creeping and intrusive among other rootlets in an upper layer of the leaf mould, shallow ever upon creviced lime rock as it is, so that a sudden downpour of rain leading to a local soil slip may easily remove a site bodily (e.g. as on Knipe's steep slope) a yard at least.'

These words, written nearly seventy years ago, go some way towards justifying the efforts of conservationists today to discourage visits to the site of the single existing plant by those whose climbing boots could do more damage than the most violent rainstorm. The present site, too, happens to be on a steep slope. Meanwhile efforts are being made, so far without success, to assist pollination and so obtain seed which will germinate into seedlings for planting out in years to come on other sites. But the chances of finding an unlooked-for stem of wild Lady's Slipper in flower in an unexpected place would seem to be fairly remote.

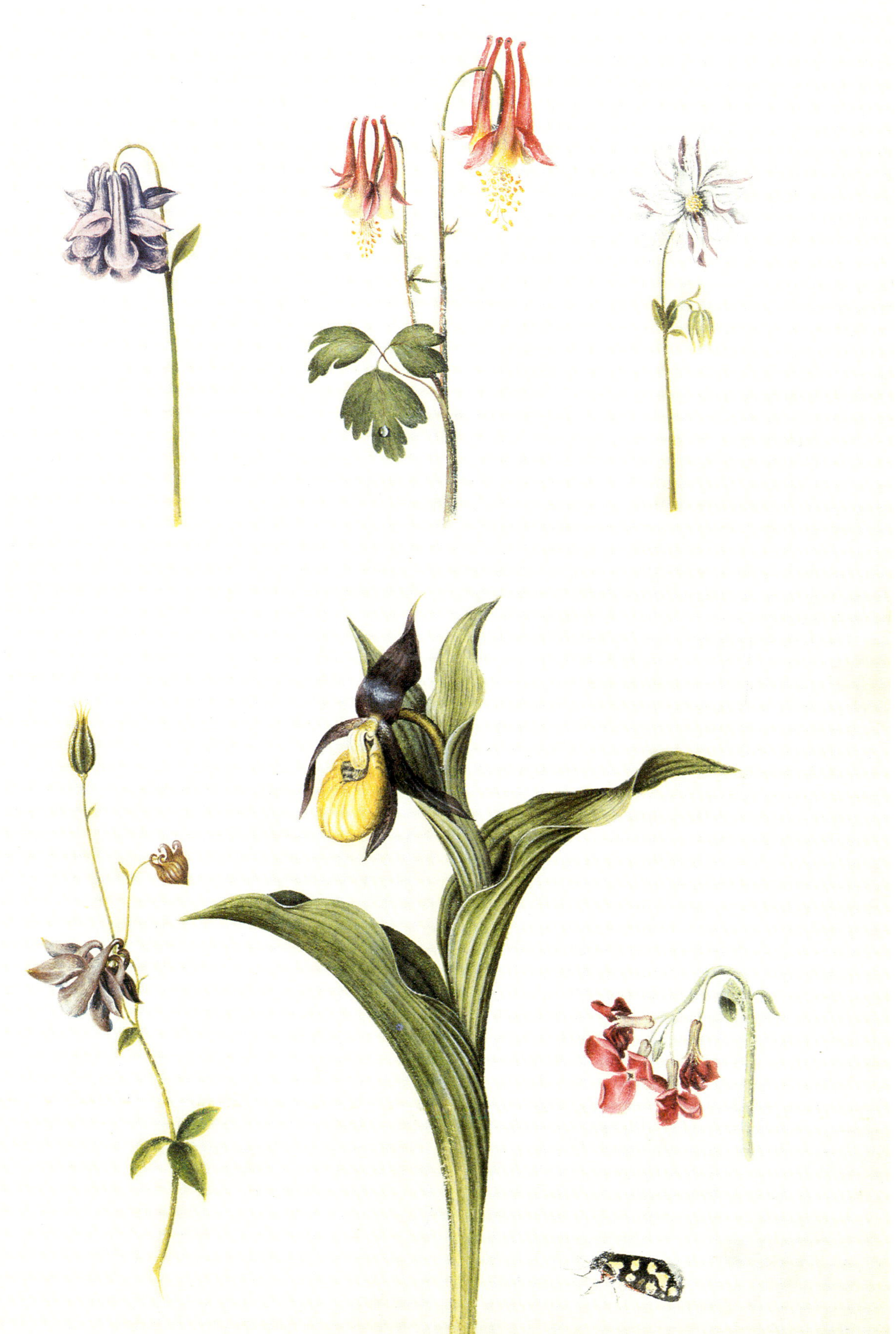

Canadian Columbine

Colombine Virigina
aquilegia virginiana
Virginie Colombine

Here we see one of the plants that appeared in John Tradescant's Garden List of 1634 but he doesn't tell us how it came to him. It must have arrived after 1629, for otherwise we should have expected to read of it in Parkinson's *Paradisi*; instead, it appears first in his *Theatrum Botanicum*, published in 1640.

In its clownish yellow and red colours *Aquilegia canadensis* seems very remote from the sober colombines of Chaucer and Shakespeare, for these would refer to our own native columbine, normally of a dark purplish-blue colour, with no variegated harlequin coloration. Nevertheless Columbine, from the Latin word for dove, is an excellent name for our wild plant. For when the flowers are in bloom, the nectaries, attached, one to each of the five petals, point to the skies, their tips curving inwards to each other in a ring. It needs but a little imagination to see them as a group of doves in conclave, cooing a descant.

But the Latin name *Aquilegia* meaning the Eagle's Flower is also apt. Those long necks stretched upward from the body of the flower could be eagles' necks, such as one sometimes sees on a lectern in church or on a coat of arms.

Canadian Columbine is shown on p.55, top left and centre, and bottom left

The plant shown here has no confidential groups of pigeons on top of its flowers. But the straight spurs of some species have an attraction of their own, especially if the flowers face upwards or sideways, for then they look like beautiful flying insects.

Columbine rose or star stripe
Aquilegia versicolor rosea sive stellata
the rose or starre stript colombin

This other unusual columbine shown on the top right of this page is not called *rosea* because of its colour, but because the structure of the flower, which is unspurred, seemed to suggest a rose that has been laid open – or even a marigold. The leaves and the rest of the plant are those of the normal columbine. The colours are as variable and mixed as those of the normal double columbines. According to Parkinson, 'it giveth seed, preserving his own kinde for the most part'.

The nearest species to be cultivated in gardens today is *Semiaquilegia ecalcarata* from western China. The foliage is fernlike, the flowers reddish purple. According to the Royal Horticultural Society's records it did not appear here until 1915. As for the other columbine (top left), which Marshal calls '*aquilegia simplex*, the single colombin', it may look unexciting, yet it has produced some of the most popular varieties for gardens today.

The moth at the foot of the page is a cream-spot Tiger (*Arctia villica*).

Everlasting Pea

Pea Everlasting, blue
Lathirus Latifolius sive pisum perenne
Pease everlasting

Here is a delightful study of the Everlasting Pea, *Lathyrus latifolius*, in which the colours are probably as vivid today as when they were first laid on paper 300 years ago.

The species, though not native to Britain, often escapes into the wild from a garden or lives on there long after the house that gave rise to its first planting has become a ruin. When at large, the plant particularly favours railway embankments as many a traveller, halted at an unscheduled stop on his way to work, will have observed.

Its cousin, the Narrow-leaved Everlasting Pea, is native here, and, in Marshal's day, was still popular in gardens. But it prefers the partial shade of a hedgerow or woodland ride, and its flowers fade if exposed to strong sunlight – a defect which may have led Marshal to prefer the introduced plant to the wild one.

Lathyrus, the genus to which the Everlasting Peas belong, is distinguished by having either angled or winged stems, the latter characteristic being shown very clearly in Marshal's painting.

The upper petal of the flowers, known as the standard, will have covered the other four petals during the bud stage, and is impressively large. The two side petals or wings are generously curved, but the two lower petals, forming the keel of the flower, behind which the stamens are concealed, are given no more emphasis than they merit. The sepals, not separated, but joined to form a tube, are represented with accuracy.

Marshal's flower had no fragrance. The Sweet-scented Pea, *Lathyrus odoratus*, which grows wild in Sicily, came later to England. It was first publicly recorded in 1697 by Father Franciscus Cupani in his work *Hortus Catholicus*, and the priest sent the seeds, two years later, to an English amateur gardener D. Robert Uvedale, master at the Grammar School at Enfield, Middlesex. Among nurserymen, however, it was a slow developer.

At flower shows today, judges are advised by the Royal Horticultural Society to mark Sweet Peas out of a total of 20 points, giving 7 points for trueness of colour and freshness of bloom, 4 points for regular placing of blooms, 6 points for size and form of bloom and 3 for length of stem in relation to the size of bloom. Fragrance is not assessed. Viewed in this light, Marshal's Everlasting Pea would, in its own class and era, surely have deserved to be rated as Highly Commended.

The Everlasting Pea is shown on p.59, top

An Iris

Iris, varigated, bulbus small
Iris angustifolio minor pannonica sive versicolor Clusii
the small variable hungarian flouerde luce of Clusius

The indexer has slipped here. Clusius's work, *Rariorum aliquot Stirpium per Pannoniam Austriam et Vicinus quasdam Provincias Observatorum*, appeared in 1583, and listed three species of *Iris angustifolia*. One of these, similar to this specimen, is described as a variety of *Iris angustifolia media*, and is illustrated with veining, said to be purple, on the falls. Unfortunately it is shown with a rhizomatous root and not a bulbous one. He also lists an *Iris angustifolia minor*, which he found growing in the fields around Vienna, Gumpoldskirchen, and Medeling, but did not describe it, as he saw no difference between it and a species already identified by Dodoens which he, Clusius, had seen for many years growing in Belgian gardens.

Parkinson knew the plant well, noting that the falls of the flower 'are variably striped with white and purple, without any thrume or fringe at all', just as in Marshal's painting. Parkinson added that the root was black and small, but his illustration did not show it as being bulbous. Mr G. Cassidy of the British Iris Society, who examined Alexander Marshal's painting, writes that the modern equivalent would be *Iris sibirica* – though of a colour not seen nowadays – one of many seventeenth-century cultivars that have since been lost.

Today, *Iris variegata* refers to an iris showing brilliant yellow flowers streaked with brown.

Scabious

Mustard of Candia
Thlaspi Candia
Candie mustard

Culpeper said of the Field Scabious: 'It grows in meadows especially around London,' so it is somewhat surprising to find it described in Marshal's sketchbook as the mustard of Candia (Crete). The confusion may have arisen because our own native candytuft, which is a member of the cress family and took its name from a Cretan near relative, *Iberis umbellata*, was at one time known as Peasant's Mustard. Elsewhere in his sketchbook Marshal shows the dark ruby *Scabiosa atropurpurea*, the Pin-cushion Plant, then, as now, a garden favourite. It is widely spread in southern Europe and not exclusive to Crete.

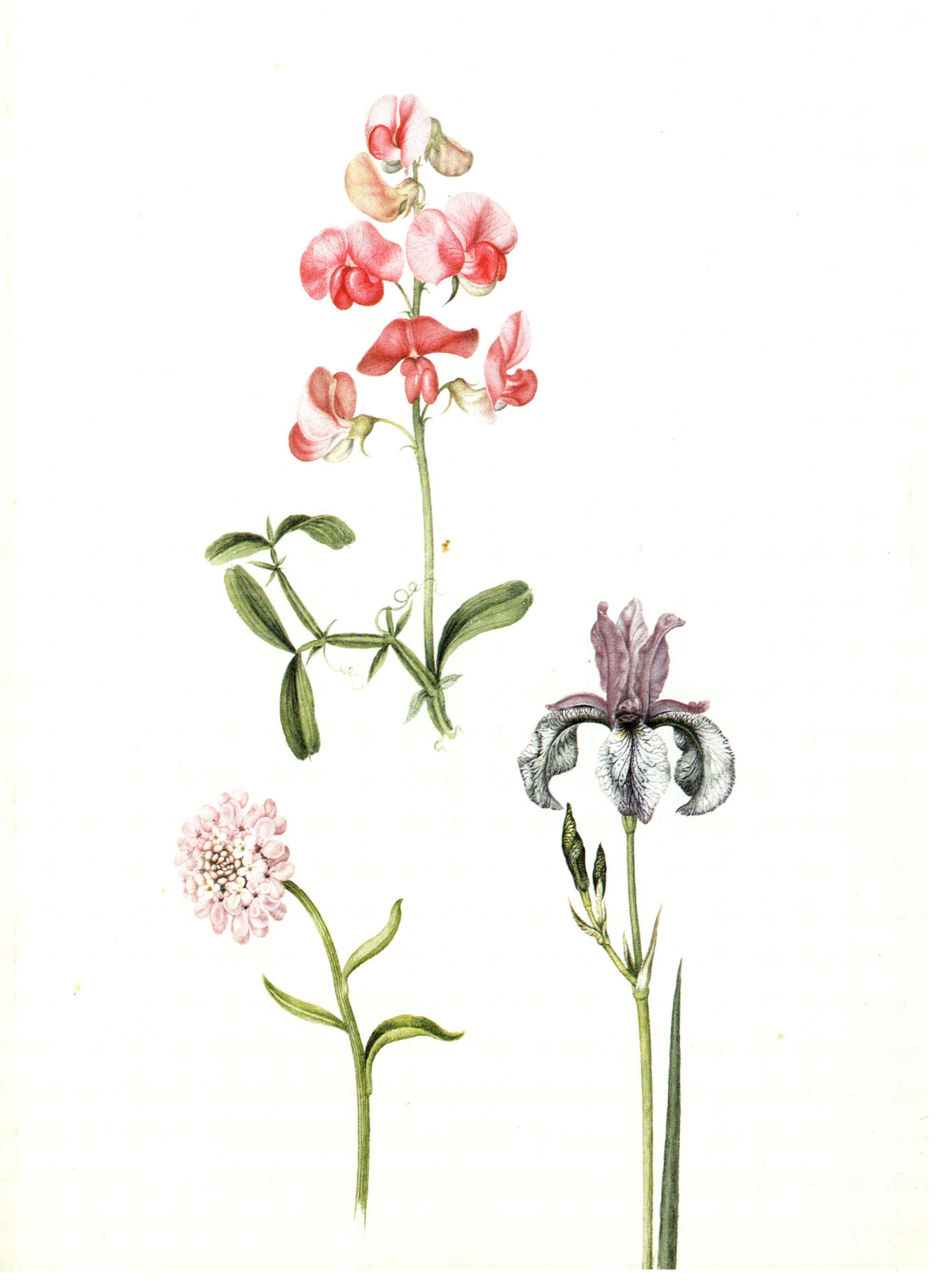
71

Paeonies

Piony double red, female
peona feamina vulgaris flore pleno rubro
the double read pionie

Where two species existed with one slightly larger or coarser than the other, the practice, in Marshal's day, was to consider the larger species male and the lesser as female. The male paeony – *Paeonia mascula* – first appears in English garden literature at the beginning of the thirteenth century, although it was probably in cultivation long before then. The female species, *Paeonia officinalis,* of which the main distinguishing characteristic is its finer leaves, should, because of its Latin name, have been the one officially sold as a remedy for, according to Culpeper, 'the falling sickness' and cleansing the womb after childbirth. 'It is also good against, melancholy dreams,' Culpeper added. The roots, he said, were of more virtue than the seed; next the flowers; and last of all the leaves. But it was not the roots of the female paeony, fresh gathered, washed clean, and stamped small, which were used for remedying prolapse, but that of the male. The female paeony remained intact to decorate the flower-bed. Here, it occupies the top half of the plate.

John Parkinson describes a double-red paeony which was almost certainly this female paeony and adds that 'like the single red paeony of Constantinople' it is 'so frequent in any garden of note, that it almost labour in vain to describe it'.

The Paeony of Constantinople (lower left) was probably *Paeonia peregrina*, i.e., the foreign paeony. The flowers are brilliant red, cup-shaped, without any of the purplish tinge attributable to the ordinary garden cultivars, and the leaves are bright green and finely cut. This is a single-petalled species and it is disappointing that Marshal chose instead to paint two versions of the double-petalled form here.

By 1667, not so long after Marshal filled his album, there would have been many more varieties from which to choose, for in that year George Rickets, a nurseryman of Hoxton, in the Hackney area of east London, produced the earliest general catalogue of a plant nursery and sent a copy to Sir Thomas Hanmer. The list included 'whit', 'blush' and 'purple' paeonies, while Sir Thomas's own *Garden Book* mentions four different doubles and six single-flowered varieties, one of which was stated to be deep mulberry-coloured, or black.

The Asian paeonies including the milky white *Paeonia lactiflora* and the lemon-coloured *Paeonia* with the tongue-twisting name of *P. mlokosewitschii* were not available in Marshal's time, and the first tree paeony, a hybrid pink form, obtained for Sir Joseph Banks, did not reach Kew till 1787.

It is uncertain which cranesbill it is that is shown. French Cranesbill, *Geranium endressi,* suits its shape and arrangement of petals, but not its colour.

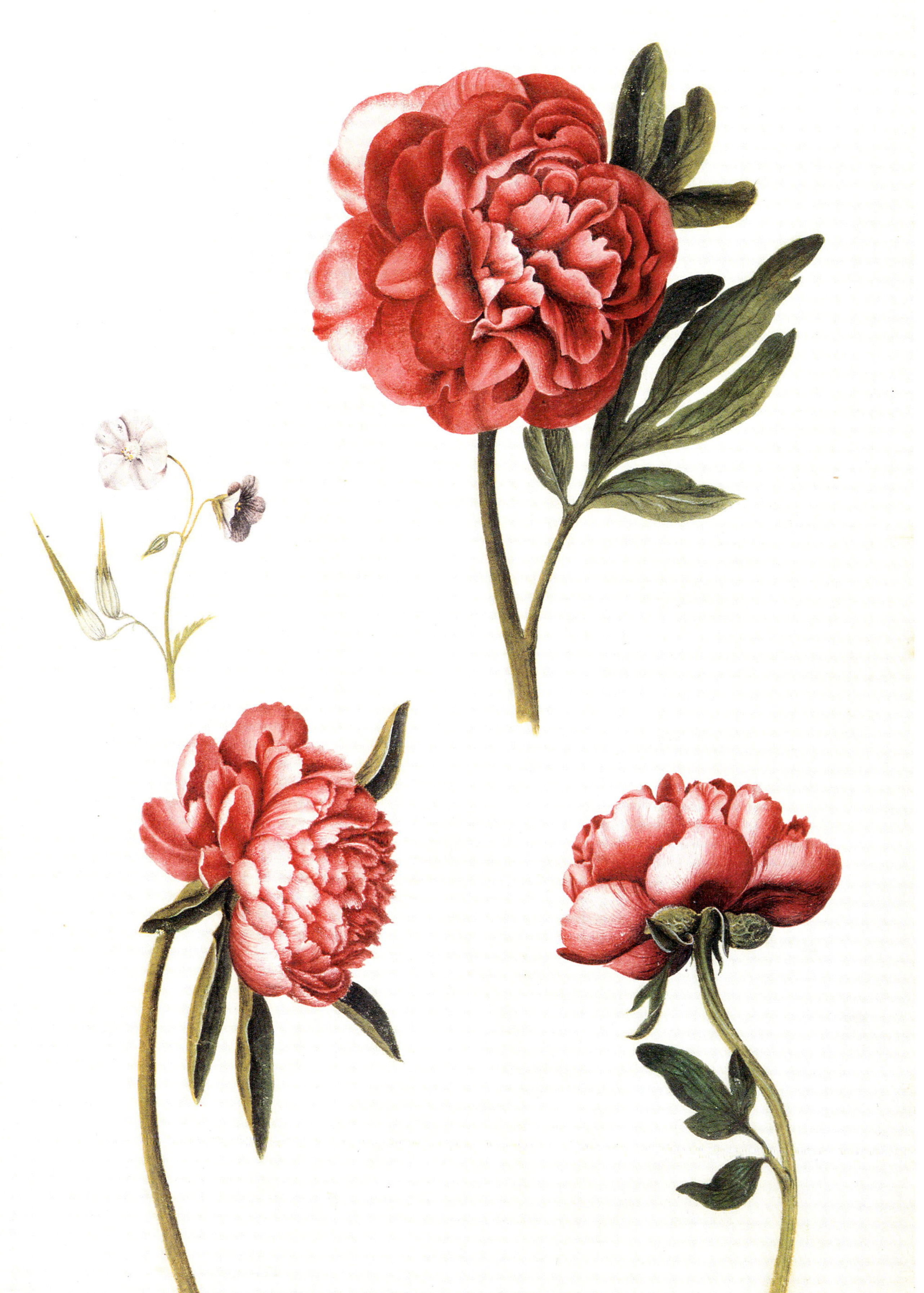

Tradescantias

Spiderwort of Virginia
phalanguim virginianum
Virginian spiderworth

The disarray and confusion to which earlier botanists were subjected are exemplified in this plant. The mischief can be traced back to the first century AD when Pedanos Dioscorides' great work *De Materia Medica* appeared. In it, he referred to a plant which he recommended as a cure for bites from scorpions or from a certain type of spider which the Greeks believed – mistakenly – to be venomous. Their name for it was, in English rendering, Phalangion. But Dioscorides' description was not sufficiently precise for gardeners to identify the plant or for the apothecaries to prepare the antidote from it. So Phalangium and spiderwort remained, as Gerard put it, a subject of much contention among later writers. Both Gerard and Parkinson show lily-type 'Spiderworts' of the ancient world in their works, but are no more precise than Dioscorides in distinguishing them from other similar plants such as the asphodels. Their illustrations point however to *Anthericum liliago*, St Bernard's Lily with its grasslike leaves and white starlike flowers with conspicuous yellow stamens. This is a member of the lily family but with tuberous roots.

When the new plant shown here arrived from Virginia, it caused a sensation; and Parkinson, to whom the cultivation of the plant had been entrusted by Tradescant, decided that it was a spiderwort – though it is not even a member of the lily family.

'This Spiderwort is of late knowledge,' Parkinson wrote in his *Paradisi in Sole*, 'For it the Christian World is indebted unto that painfull and industrious searcher, and lover of all nature's varieties John Tradescant (sometimes belonging to [i.e. working for] the right Honourable Lord Robert Earle of Salisbury, Lord Treasurer of England in his time, and then unto the right Honourable the Lord Wotton at Canterbury in Kent, and lastly unto the late Duke of Buckingham) who first received it of a friend, that brought it out of Virginia, thinking it to bee the Silke Grasse that groweth there. . . .'

This would have referred to John Tradescant senior. As the King's gardener and a member of the Virginia Company, from 1617 he was able to procure a fine stock of plants from America and some forty of them are named in his garden book of 1634 – including the Virginian Spiderwort which, as is clear, Parkinson must already have grown before 1629.

Parkinson did not, however, overpraise the plant and noted that the 'flower openeth it selfe in the day & shutteth usually at night, and never openeth againe, but perisheth'. He confessed that he had himself imposed the name *Phalangium ephemerum Virginianum Ioannis Tradescanti* to hold until someone found a better one. As the English translation he gave: 'The Soon Fading Spiderwort of Virginia, or Tradescant, his Spiderwort'.

But should Tradescant have received so much credit for introducing the soon-fading spiderwort? It seems not; for, as Wilfrid Blunt pointed out in *The Art of Botanical Illustration* Georg Hoefnagel, who died in 1600, and had finished his great work, *Missale Romanum*, ten years earlier, included a painting of the very same plant. Moreover Gerard, in the second edition of his *Herbal*, published in 1633, recalled that Gaspard Bauhin described it in his *Pinax Theatri Botanici* published ten years earlier. Hoefnagel worked in Munich, Vienna, Prague and in the Tirol; Bauhin though born of a French father spent most of his life in Basle. So it would seem that the plant enjoyed a wide circulation on the continent.

The English, after all, did not have North America to themselves. At the time Marshal painted his flower portraits, the Dutch were still established in New Amsterdam, the New York of the future. Champlain had founded Quebec in 1608,

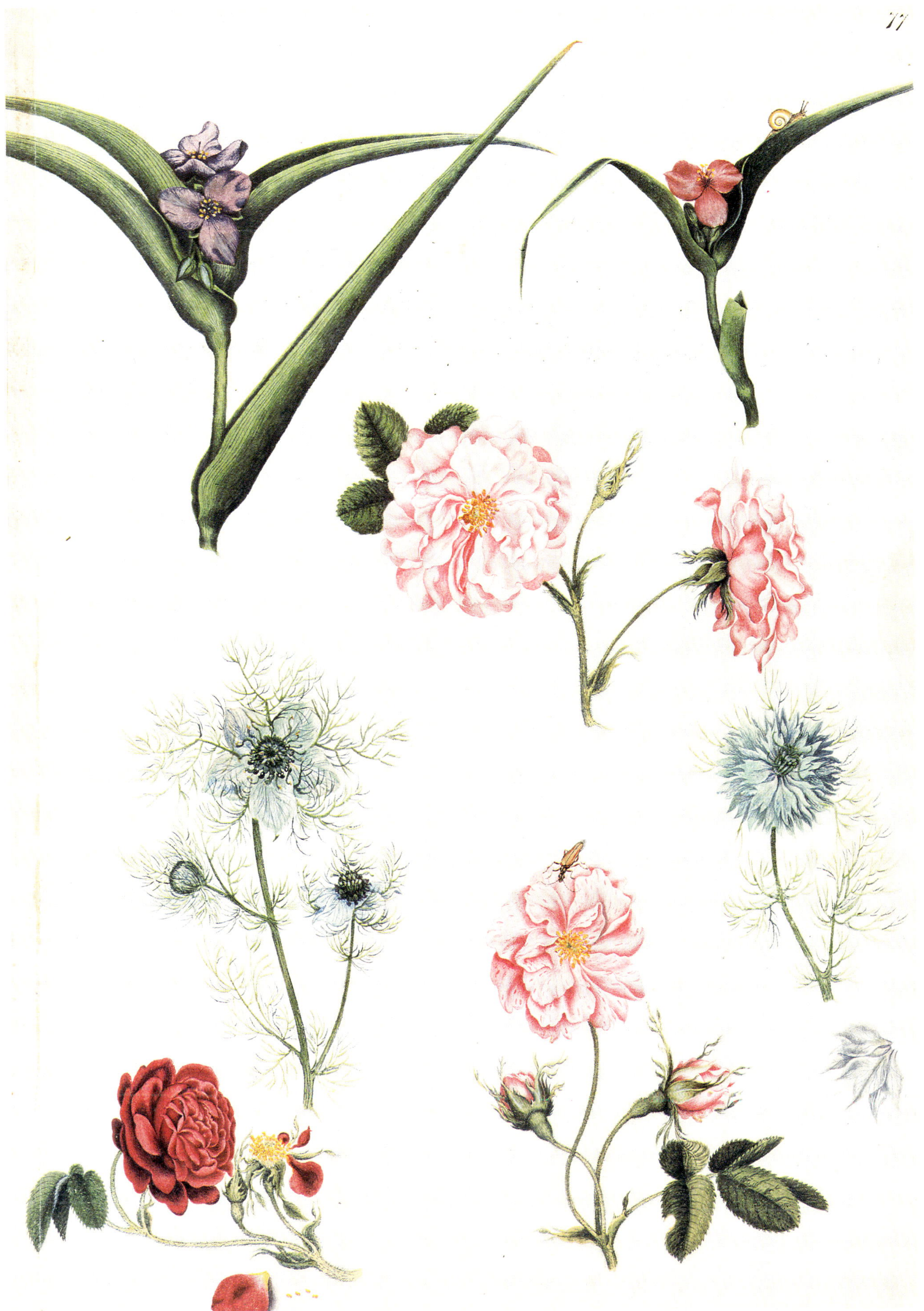

and the French occupied Canada for nearly a century and a half. Some of the French Canadian plants appear in Jean Cornu's *Histoire des Plantes*; they were provided by Vespasien Robin who worked as botanical demonstrator under Guy de la Brosse, the very first Keeper of the Jardin du Roi. So, in one way or another, many American plants could have been circulating in Europe before they crossed the Channel to England.

A Miscellany

This plate shows Marshal at his most versatile. It also shows single and double *Nigella* – Love-in-a-Mist – called in those days the Fennel Flower, because of its fennel-like leaves.

In mid-page there is the frilly-petalled 'Regatte Rose'. One is left in doubt as to whether the name denoted 'Ragged Rose' or whether like the Venetian word 'regatta' it meant, as the *O.E.D.* puts it, 'struggling for the maistrie'. The flowers are very much like Redouté's *Rosa damascena Italica* (Volume III folio 37).

The Rose at the foot of the page (centre) and described as 'The Speckled Rose of hungarie' seems to agree with John Parkinson's Hungarian Rose 'finely spotted with faint spots as it were spread over the red'. Redouté's *Rosa gallica flore marmoreo* (Vol III folio 49) also has spotted petals – in that case pink spots on maroon.

The dark red rose was known then as *Rosa holoserica*, the Velvet Rose, because its deep colour recalled that of crimson velvet. It was almost thornless and its modern equivalent would be the *Gallica* type known as Tuscany.

A Miscellany is shown on p.63

The Hemisphere Rose

Rose, yellow double
Rosa lutea multiplex sive flore pleno
The double yeleo rose

Two yellow roses had reached Britain by 1625. One was the so-called Austrian Briar which had single-petalled flowers like those of our own wild rose. (It was originally known as *Rosa lutea*, but, because its buttercup yellow blossoms emit a strong odour, unpleasant to some, it was renamed *Rosa foetida*.) The other yellow rose is seen here. It was quite natural for Marshal to call it the multiplex or double-flowered yellow rose. It soon, however, achieved a more distinctive description – *Rosa hemisphaerica*.

Both the double yellow rose and the Austrian Briar came originally from Persia. They were mentioned by Clusius in his survey of German gardens, published in 1583, but the way in which *Rosa hemisphaerica* was discovered, or rather uncovered, provides a scintilla of garden history. While in Vienna, Clusius happened to see a model, executed in miniature, of a garden in Constantinople. In it was an unfamiliar flower – a double yellow rose. Some gardeners might have assumed that the model maker had taken artistic licence – and would have dismissed the matter from their minds. But Clusius made enquiries, found that a double yellow rose did, indeed, exist, and managed to get hold of one.

Unfortunately the blooms are easily damaged by rain and in addition the gardeners of the day found the variety difficult to grow. Parkinson reported that two of the plants introduced to England had perished, and Sir Thomas Hanmer complained that this rose did not 'blow' (bloom) well and that the buds seem to be eaten by worms, though this is clearly not the case with Marshal's bloom which has opened unusually wide. Other painters, in particular Jan van Huysum whose crowded set-flower pieces are to be seen in so many official galleries, found, or perhaps interpolated, unblemished petals.

On looking at this page of Marshal's work, Mr E. F. Allen, Past President of the Royal National Rose Society and a Member of its Council, wrote: 'This is a good painting of an *Alba* rose and very close to the one which we now know as *Alba Maxima*. Below is a very good painting of *R. hemisphaerica Herrm.* and better than that by Alfred Parsons in Ellen Willmott's *Genus Rosa*, No. 93 (1910–14). We grow and flower this Rose every year; it is much easier to flower than is suggested by many old authors. Redouté's painting of this Rose is too exaggerated and many Dutch and Flemish painters have made the same error.'

The Hemisphere Rose is shown on p.67, bottom

English Rose

Rose, White English
rosa anglica alba
The whit English rose

Marshal has rightly given this double rose pride of place. The single form of this is the White Rose of York, which, like the Rose of Minden, and for that matter the Plantagenets' Broom, has its place in the history books. Furthermore, although in the long run our hedgerow Dog Rose has played but a small part in the development of the nurseryman's rose, it is generally believed that the English Rose sprang from an ancient hybrid between the Dog Rose, *Rosa canina*, and the Apothecaries' Rose – *Rosa gallica*. But it also has some of the characteristics of *Rosa phoenicia* which would link it with the Damask Rose – again with *Rosa canina* as the other parent.

The true English Rose does not blush over its past, but Marshal has correctly shown the hint of gold which appears as the buds open and which changes to pure white as the flower expands. The thorns, too, are characteristically formed – large, hooked, and fairly remote from one another. The bloom is dish-shaped and the leaflets have a bluish tinge, which helps to distinguish the variety from most others. Given more space, Marshal would surely have shown us the impressive structure of the whole plant. Left to its own devices, it forms a large bush and is a vigorous climber. It is extremely hardy and requires little attention, which helps to explain its current popularity at a time when more and more attention is being paid to 'old-fashioned' shrub roses.

Marshal named the campanula on the left of the page '*Rapuntium parvum*, small rampion', and it would seem to be our *Campanula rapunculus*, Rampion Bellflower – an introduced plant which grows wild in Britain though it is rare and local.

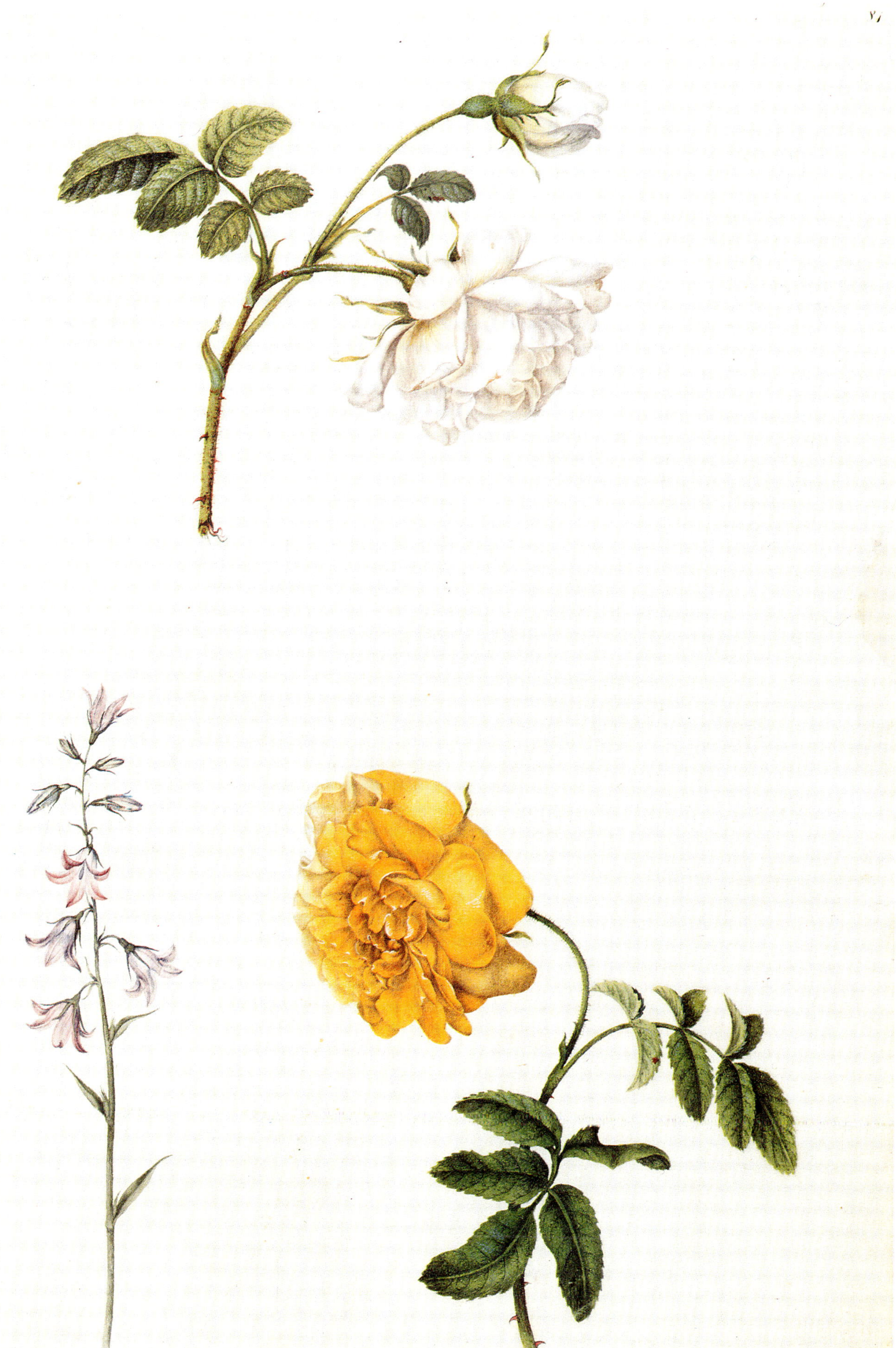

The Hundred-Leaved Rose

Rose of Province
Rosa provincialis

Referred to by Herodotus as having sixty 'leaves' and unsurpassed fragrance – and by Theophrastus as the rose with a hundred 'leaves', was this the same Cabbage Rose as that which appeared in Britain towards the end of the sixteenth century? Here, in Marshal's album we see some at least of its characteristic features, the glands on the stalks from which fragrance is dispensed, and the leaves and flowers drooping characteristically. Marshal could have shown the thorns of varying sizes.

Edward Bunyard, scholar and rosarian, refers in his book, *Old Garden Roses*, to a rhyming puzzle devised probably by the monks of the Middle Ages, which invited the reader to guess which family was referred to in the following lines:

We are brothers at the same time borne.
Two of us have beards, by two no beards are worn
While one, lest he should give his brothers pain,
Has one side bearded and the other plain.

The jingle was particularly appropriate to the Cabbage Rose, because the five brothers were the five sepals enclosing the bud of the flower. Two of these are fully enclosed and can therefore grow no beards on their edges. Two more of the sepals have edges which are not enclosed and can therefore grow beards, and from this it follows that the fifth sepal has one external and one internal edge and can therefore grow only half a beard.

Though regarded by Linnaeus as a species, the Cabbage Rose is probably a hybrid product of more than one wild species.

The name *Rosa provincialis* used by Marshal and others for this rose, has caused some confusion. *Provincialis* applied originally to a territory outside Italy which had been brought under Roman government, and was thus often applied to Provence. But the evidence is that the Cabbage Rose developed more particularly in the Netherlands and the adjective might even have referred to the United Provinces of the Netherlands formed in 1579. Of these provinces Holland was by far the richest and most important, which, perhaps, led to Clusius's acceptance of a professorship at Leyden, and to the Cabbage Rose being called, by some, the Provincial Rose of Holland.

A further complication arose from the fact that the small fortified town of Provins, some sixty miles south-east of Paris, had for many years been the centre of rose cultivation, particularly *Rosa gallica officinalis*, the Apothecaries Rose. In the eighteenth century *Rosa provincialis* was used as a synonym for this rose, and this led many mistakenly to call the Cabbage Rose not merely the Rose of Provence, but the Rose of Provins. Today, praise be, the Cabbage Rose is no longer *R. provincialis*, but *R. centifolia* in deference to the profusion of petals.

Valuable if critical comment by Mr E. F. Allen: 'Two very fine paintings of *Centifolia* Roses. The flowers are less exaggerated than paintings by Redouté; the leaves not quite so well painted as by Ehret.'

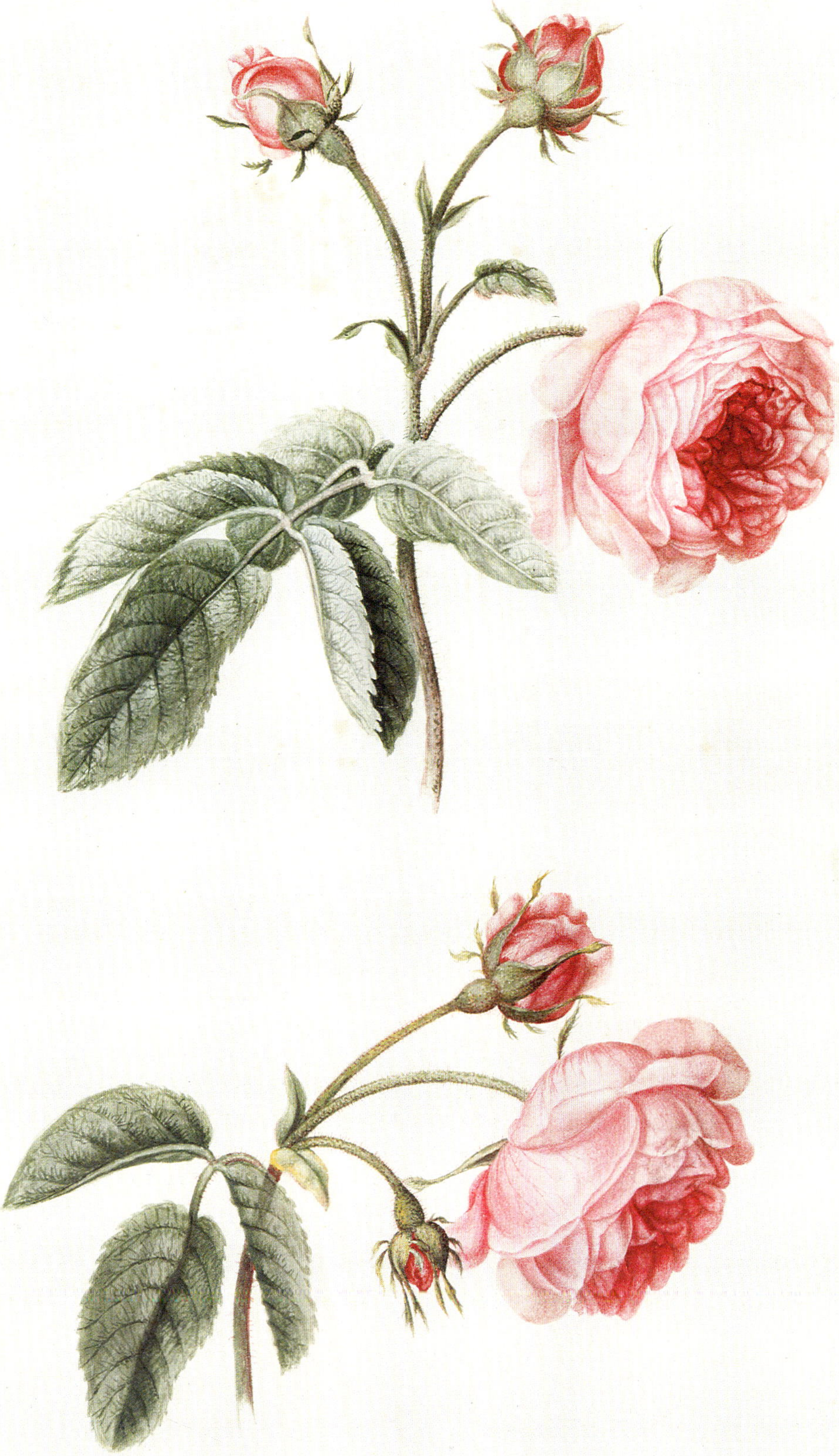

The Campanulas

Coventry bells
viola mariana flore purpoereo
Coventry bels or marion violet

This portrait of a campanula is one of eight painted by Marshal in this album. It is well described by Parkinson, who noted that the plant was a biennial, that the leaves were a little hairy all over, and the stalks somewhat hairy also. 'At the end of every branch stand the flowers,' he wrote, 'in green huskes, from whence come large round hollow bels, swelling out in the middle and rising somewhat about it, like the necks of a pot, and then ending in fine corners, which are either of a faire or faint white, or of a pale blew purplish colour, and sometimes of a deeper purple or violet.' Clearly the Coventry Bell of Parkinson's day is the Canterbury Bell (*Campanula medium*) of today. The decision to make the change-over was apparently taken after the end of the seventeenth century, which makes it more likely that this is one of Marshal's own identifications. The 'Canterbury Bells' of Marshal's day were of two kinds. One, the '*Trachelium maius* or the Great Canterbury Bels or Throatewort' had 'many large rough leaves somewhat like unto Nettle leaves, being broad and round at the bottom, with the flowers somewhat lesser than those of the Coventry Bell'. This is a recognizable portrait of the modern *Campanula trachelium*, the Nettle-leaved Bellflower, sometimes known as 'Bats in the Belfry'. It is a native plant, but striking enough to be worth cultivating if the soil is sufficiently alkaline. The seventeenth-century *Trachelium minus*, known as 'the Small throateworte or Canterbury bells' bore flowers that grew 'in a bulb or tuft thicke set together'. In other words it was today's *Campanula glomerata*, the Clustered Bellflower.

Parkinson also mentioned another species which bore the name *Trachelium giganteum* – the Giant's Throatworte. This may have been *Campanula latifolia* which can grow to nearly four feet, though Parkinson thought at the time that it was no taller than other campanulas in his garden and that the epithet *giganteum* had been given merely for 'difference sake'. Nevertheless the English name for *Campanula latifolia* remains Giant Bellflower.

Marshal also included elsewhere the Peach-leaved Bellflower, *Campanula persicifolia*, better described as the Narrow-leaved Bellflower. It is an introduced species from Europe, a church spire of a plant which also forms mats. It is often cultivated in gardens, but has successfully established itself in a wild state in the south of England. Its leaves are spectacularly sword-like and the blossoms are shallow bowls of mauvish blue with a hint of turn-back at the brim.

Elsewhere in Marshal's album the *Campanula minor* or Little Purple Bellflower is to be found. This is the Bluebell of Scotland and the Harebell of the Sassenachs. Botanists have named this species *Campanula rotundifolia*, though only the lowest leaves, usually hidden beneath the foliage of surrounding plants, can pass muster as being rotund.

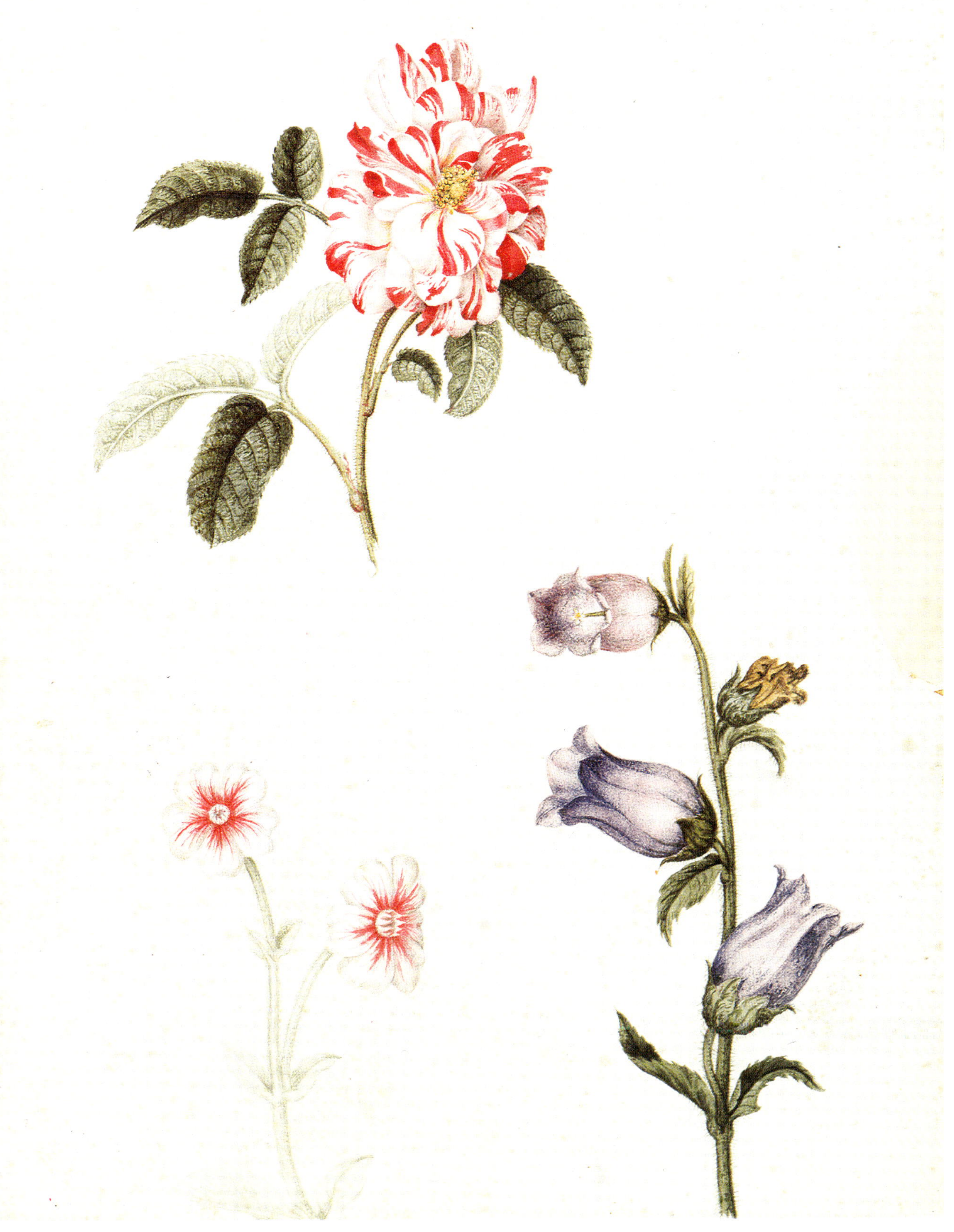
88

A Further Miscellany

The red and white rose (shown, top left) is described as '*Rossa mundi* – The rose of the World' and is a far more striking representation of this cultivar than Redouté's portrait of *Rosa gallica versicolor* a century later. This variety is a sport of *Rosa gallica*. Many writers, including Parkinson, have confused the rose on this page with the Rose of York and Lancaster – *Rosa damascena versicolor* – a pale pink rose, blotched rather than striped with red. It is derived from the Summer Damask Rose.

The third flower on this page 'Rose Striped Champion – *Lichnis Coronnaria versicolor* – the stript rose Campion' is a variety of our old friend the Rose Campion with the silvery lamb's-wool foliage, a garden plant in England since the mid-fourteenth century. But this striped-awning variety must have been particularly tempting to paint.

These flowers are to be found on p.71

Some Larkspurs

Larkspur, double blue upright
delfinium multiplex elatius flore pleno diversorum colorum
double Larkshilles

Three species of larkspur had been introduced into England before Marshal painted this portrait of one of them. The first to be noticed appeared in 1551 in a list prepared by the Tudor botanist William Turner for his book *The New Herball*. This gave the 'Names of Herbes' in Greek, Latin, Dutch, and French as well as in English. In it he referred to 'Stavesacre' which we know more formally as *Delphinium staphisagria* – a plant which carries one of the most inappropriate of botanical names, since *staphis agria* is the Greek for 'wild raisin'. The plant was grown in medicinal gardens – particularly in Italy – for its seeds, which yielded an alkaloid poison effective, in small doses, for alleviating tooth-ache, and a powder which could drive vermin out of children's hair. The flowers are distinguished by their very short spurs.

Then there was *Delphinium consolida*, Branching Larkspur, which sometimes appears wild in Britain as a casual in corn-fields, especially in those near ports, displaying widely spreading branches but only a modest quota of flowers.

Here, however, Marshal was depicting another introduced species, the erect and less branched *Delphinium ambiguum*, known simply as larkspur, which is a favourite in gardens and occasionally naturalized outside them. Like the two preceding species, it is an annual and, though its flowers are normally bright blue, they can turn out pink or white, which makes *ambiguum* meaning 'changeable' a suitable description for it. Marshal includes a pink variety in his album.

In all delphiniums both the petals of the flower and the sepals behind them are arranged spirally, and, in addition, the sepals resemble petals, so that the blooms present a somewhat dishevelled appearance. Parkinson, in describing the 'Double upright Larkes heeles of many colours' says that 'there appeare many flowers upon the stalkes . . . layd or spread broade open, as the Rose Columbine, without any heeles behind them, very delightfull to behold, consisting of many small leaves [petals] growing together. . . .' His illustration of this variety does, indeed, show flowers without spurs even in bud. In Marshal's painting on the other hand, the heeles or spurs are evident.

In the normal larkspur the nectaries of the flower are united behind the petals into a three-lobed tube or limb, ending in a long spur which fits into the protective cover provided by the hindmost sepal. In theory the nectar can be reached only by bees with long 'tongues'; but in practice those with shorter tongues have been known to raid the nectar store by piercing the spur from the outside, without submitting to the formalities of the front door.

Mythologists linked this plant with Ajax, the Greek hero of the Trojan War, because the notches on the limb leading to the spur were thought to resemble the letters AIA. The name delphinium was bestowed on this branch of the buttercup family because, as Marshal shows, the buds of the plant suggest the figure of a dolphin.

The Larkspur is shown on p.75, right

Also on this page is what Marshal describes as 'the Purple Damask Rose', a description confirmed by Mr E. F. Allen's comment: 'The downy grey-green leaves, and the curved, reddish spines suggest a Damask Rose, but one that cannot now be matched. In 1848 William Paul listed 87 named varieties. They are one of the oldest groups of the Old Roses but many have now disappeared.'

The fallen nasturtium blossoms show features all too often neglected by the more cosmetically minded flower portrait painters, and the shading of the carnation confirms emphatically that Marshal was a right-handed painter, who worked, as is the tradition, with subjects lit from the left-hand side.

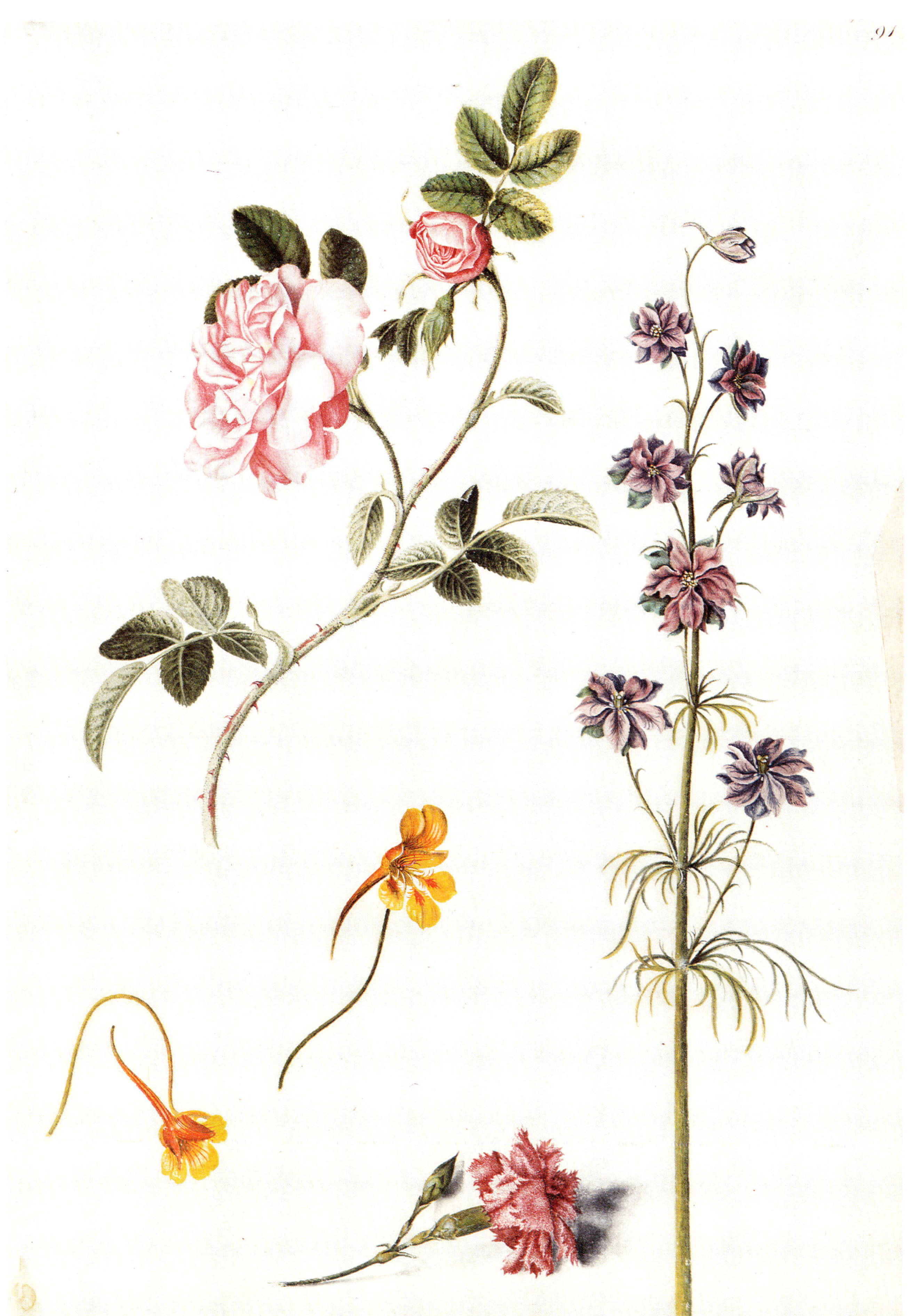

Common Toadflax

Flax, great toad flax
Linaria vulgaris lutea–
great tode flax

Once again Marshal has taken an uncultivated plant and has produced a portrait on the left which might well have caused gardeners to think twice. Probably they took for granted that a plant that grew so freely on waste ground throughout England (and from Norway to Greece) was hardly worthy of the husbandman's attention. And there were already yellow forms of the garden antirrhinum or snapdragon which but for the fact that its flowers have no spur, somewhat resembles the humble toadflax.

Gerard, however, found space for it in his *Herbal*, and compared it to the larkspur. 'The whole plant before it come to floure so much resembleth Esula minor [a spurge] that the one is hardly knowne from the other but by this old verse:

Esula lactescit
Sine lacte Linaria crescit

(Esula with milke doth flow
Toadflax without milke doth grow)'

The Toadflax is shown on the lower left

The Day Lily

Lilly, Day
Lilium non bolbosum phoeniceum
the day lillie

Although Gerard used the same name as Marshal for this fine plant, the old herbalist rightly distinguished it from the lilies proper and classed it already as *Hemerocallis*, a name which, as he points out, had been in use by herbalists for centuries. The nearest species today would probably be *Hemerocallis fulva*.

Painting the likeness of a Day Lily demands eternal vigilance of the artist, as Gerard's description hints: 'The floures be like the white Lillie in shape, of an Orenge tawny colour: of which floures much might be said which I omit. But in briefe, this plant bringeth forth in the morning his bud, which at noon is full blowne, or spred abroad, and the same day in the evening it shuts it selfe, and in a short time after becomes as rotten and stinking as if it beene trodden in a dunghill in a moneth together, in foule and rainie weather: which is the cause that the seed seldome followes, as in the other of his kinde, not bringing forth any at all that I could ever observe; according to the old proverbe, Soone ripe, soone rotten. His roots are like the former.'

Even today, few people would attempt to grow it from seed. But it is a plant, which once established comes up year after year and in this sense is anything but ephemeral.

The adjective *phoeniceum* indicates, not surprisingly, that the plant was thought to have come from Phoenicia, that part of the coast of Syria which at that time included the ports of Tyre and Sidon, through which much of the trade between Europe and the Levant passed. It was also a reasonable assumption since it was in schools in Aleppo and Damascus that the lore assembled by pre-Christian botanists such as Theophrastus and Dioscorides was translated from Greek into Arabic and preserved by the 'Phoenicians' through the Dark Ages that followed

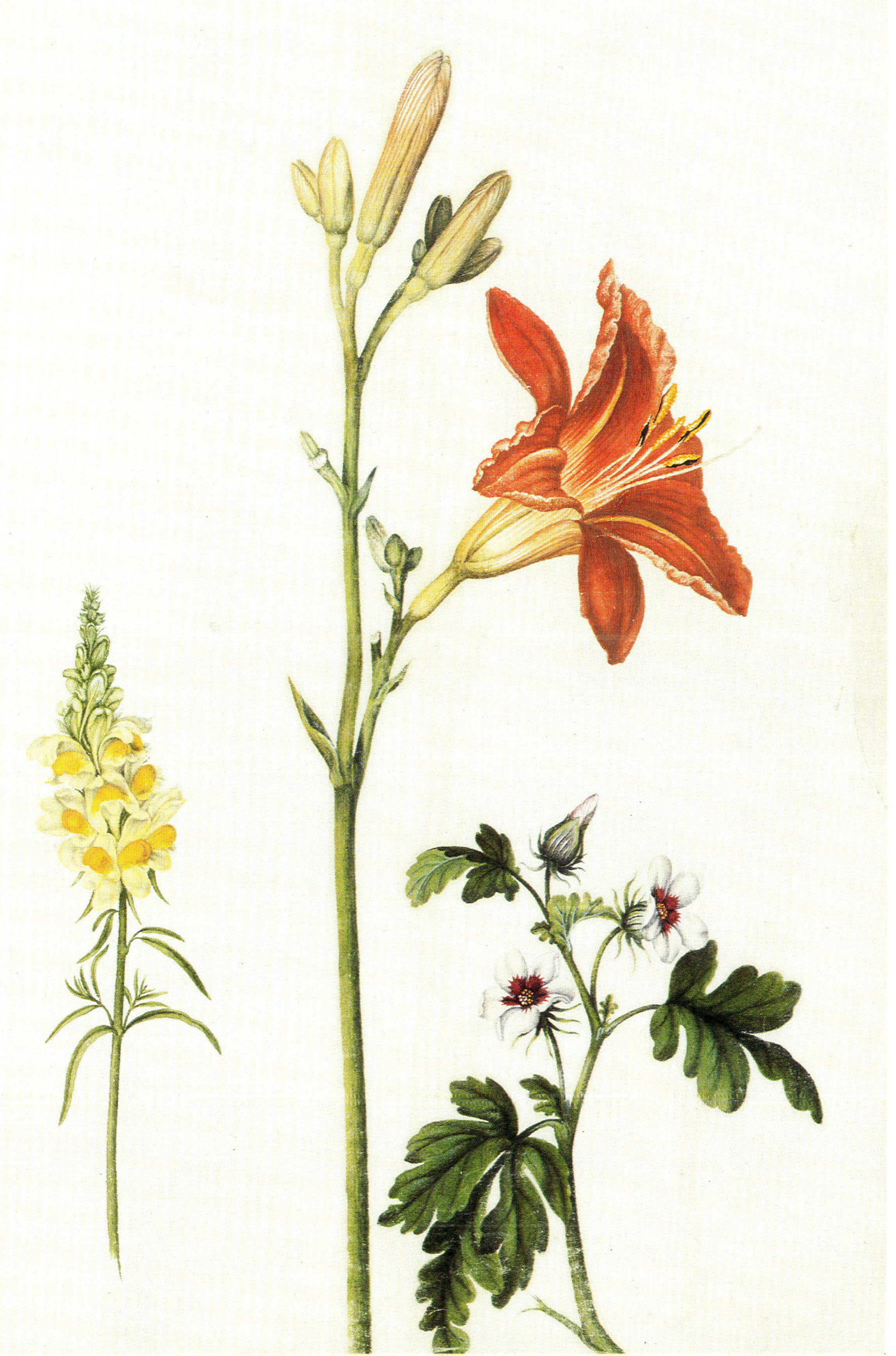

the fall of the Greek and Roman Empires. Today, however, *Hemerocallis fulva* is considered to be a native of Japan.

The attractive plant to the lower right of the page has something in common with the Day Lily. It is *Malva horaria*, the Time-keeping Mallow, so-called because the flowers close early in the day before the sun gets high enough to warm them. Parkinson especially admired the 'pestle or clapper' in the centre of the flower, which he rated was 'yellow as gold', but understandably it is not much grown in gardens.

The Two Caterpillars

The Two Caterpillars

Although page 102 of Marshal's album shows several interesting flowers – notably 'a Marygold African double', 'French March' (a double form of our own equally miscalled Marsh Marigold), a Saxifrage labelled 'Spoted Sanicle' and *Hedysarum Clypeatum* 'the Read Satin Flouer' whose spikes of reddish pea-flowers are seldom seen today – the main interest lies in the two caterpillars at the foot of the page.

Marshal did not identify these but they are those of the Puss Moth, *Dicranura vinula*, a large, not uncommon whitish moth, of which both the body and thorax are covered with Persian-cat silken fluff. The caterpillars – or caterpillar if we assume that a single model was used for both studies – are in the fifth and final skin to be carried before it turns into a chrysalis, and this may have accounted for some fading in the colours which are normally bright apple-green and lavender-purple. The horny 'shell-head' which the caterpillar carries in this stage of development is clearly shown, and also the red threadlike organs extended from the insect's twin tails. These are normally in evidence only when the caterpillar considers itself threatened for example by an Ichneumon fly endeavouring to deposit an egg in its body.

Clearly visible in the forepart of the caterpillar are the six true legs which will persist in the moth after the temporary soft-shoe locomotors of the caterpillar have been dispensed with. Two words scribbled on the verso of the page are of some interest. They are 'mange sauls' indicating correctly that the caterpillars feed on willow. If Marshal himself had provided this information of his own knowledge he would have written it in English which was his first language. If, on the other hand, some French speaker had imparted this piece of intelligence, he would have found it natural to note the fact just as it came to him without bothering to translate it into English.

There would have been no shortage at that time of French speakers who would have been interested in Marshal's paintings, and glad to be able to converse with him in their own language. One of these would have been André Mollet who had been gardener to King Charles II's mother Henrietta Maria and was still working at Wimbledon with his son Gabriel, when the king returned to the throne in 1660. Mollet had already published his work, *Le Jardin de Plaisir*, in 1651. But a more likely candidate would have been the Marshal of France, Godefroi Louis, Comte d'Estrade. He was the French ambassador at the Court of King Charles II who persuaded that monarch, for a suitable payment, to return the port of Dunkirk to France. We know that the ambassador survived Marshal by three years, and that he offered to buy the album from his widow, so he would most probably have inspected his work during the artist's lifetime.

Perhaps, without taking too much licence, we may picture the two men sitting together, side by side, with Marshal turning over the leaves on which his flower portraits were painted, making notes, while His Excellency confirmed that Ragged Robins were *Cuidrelles* as well as *Coucou* in France, and gave his views on the diet of the Puss Moth caterpillar.

The illustrations are shown on p.81

The Two Caterpillars

The little Saxifrage at the right-hand side of the page looks at first sight like London Pride but answers more closely to the description of *Saxifraga umbrosa*, an introduced plant without an English name. In the wild, it is established only at Heseldon Gill, Yorkshire, where it was first noticed in 1792. Marshal has drawn only one leaf from the tuft at the base of the plant, but has shown it with his usual accuracy. The leaf has rounded blunt scalloping on the edges, is wedge-shaped at the base and almost truncated at the tip. The main stalk is reddish and the petals ellipse-shaped with a single yellow spot and several smaller reddish ones. The fruit is reddish too.

London Pride which is of unknown origin, and not known in the wild, is a hybrid between *S. umbrosa* and *S. spathularis* which is known as St Patrick's Cabbage and does grow wild in Ireland. It has leaves edged with sharp teeth.

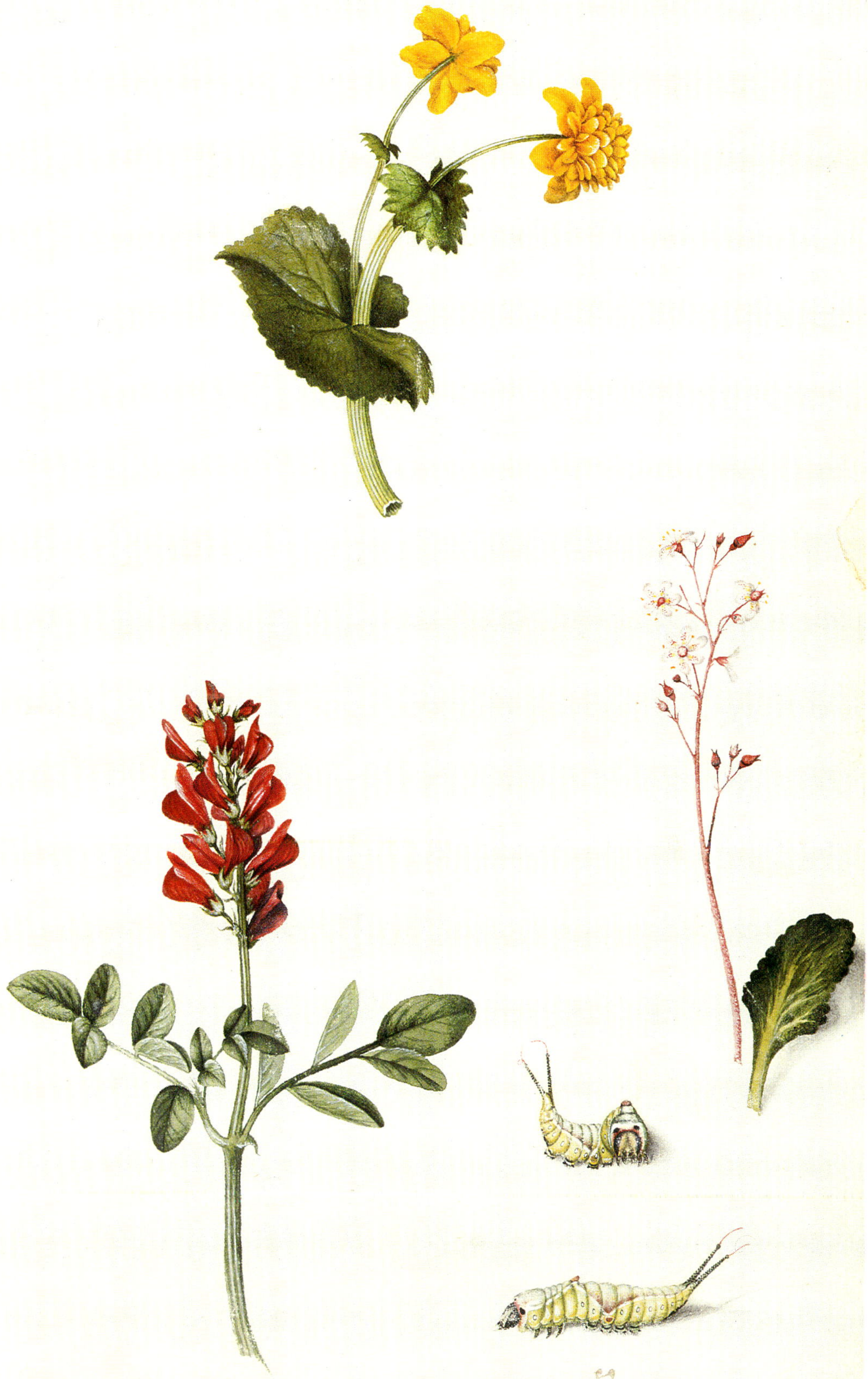

A 'Nasturtium'

Larkspur, Indian cress
nasturtium indicum
Indian cress or yealeo Larkshille

We still call this plant (shown top right) 'Nasturtium' although the word is the botanical term for watercress. Its real name is *Tropaeolum*. What gardeners of the past did carry in their minds was that its leaves tasted as sharp as any piece of watercress, and its flowers bore a spur similar to that of the larkspur even though much larger.

Nasturtium seeds gathered before they harden up have long been used as a substitute for the seeds of the caper, *Capparis spinosa*, a shrub which grows wild in the south of Europe. The best capers come from the Bouches-du-Rhône and Var areas of southern France, and it is the flower buds, small and round, which are pickled and used to sharpen up the already flavoursome Provençale grillades. But those who could not afford them could produce an acceptable relish in a few minutes by boiling up a broth of nasturtium seeds mixed with vinegar, ginger, mace, nutmeg, horse-radish and cloves.

In England caper (or nasturtium seed) sauce was traditionally served with boiled mutton, and for this reason, despite its brave show of colour, the plant was more often to be found in the vegetable patch than in the formal pleasure garden. Today, however, seeds for 'caper sauce' would not be taken from the plant we see here, for it has become almost a museum piece and is seldom grown in gardens. Where present, it can be recognized, as Marshal shows, by the distinct point visible half way round the edge of each petal.

Instead, we have *Tropaeolum majus* which was first seen in England about a quarter of a century after Marshal assembled the paintings in his album. It is from this species that breeders have derived both the 'Gleam' series and the less unruly Tom Thumbs.

The two *Tropaeolums* are native to Latin America and the Spaniards, who within twenty years had extended their empire to include Mexico, Costa Rica, Panama, Nicaragua, Guatemala, Honduras, Ecuador, Peru, Venezuela and Florida, brought back not only the Indian Cress, but other plants painted by Marshal, in particular *Mirabilis jalapa*, the Marvel of Peru. This was the plant that so deeply impressed Gerard who wrote of its petals 'glittering oftimes with a fine purple or crimson colour many times of an horse-flesh, sometimes yellow, sometimes pale and sometimes resembling an old red or yellow colour . . . having sometime great, sometime little spots of a purple colour sprinkled and scattered in a most variable order and brave mixture.'

Marshal's two paintings, on pages 147 and 148 of his album (for which we have no space), do not disappoint, but it is disillusioning to learn that the Marvel of Peru is not the source of jalap, the purgative named after a Mexican city, which comes instead from the roots of an unrelated convolvulus, *Exogonium (Ipomoea) purga*.

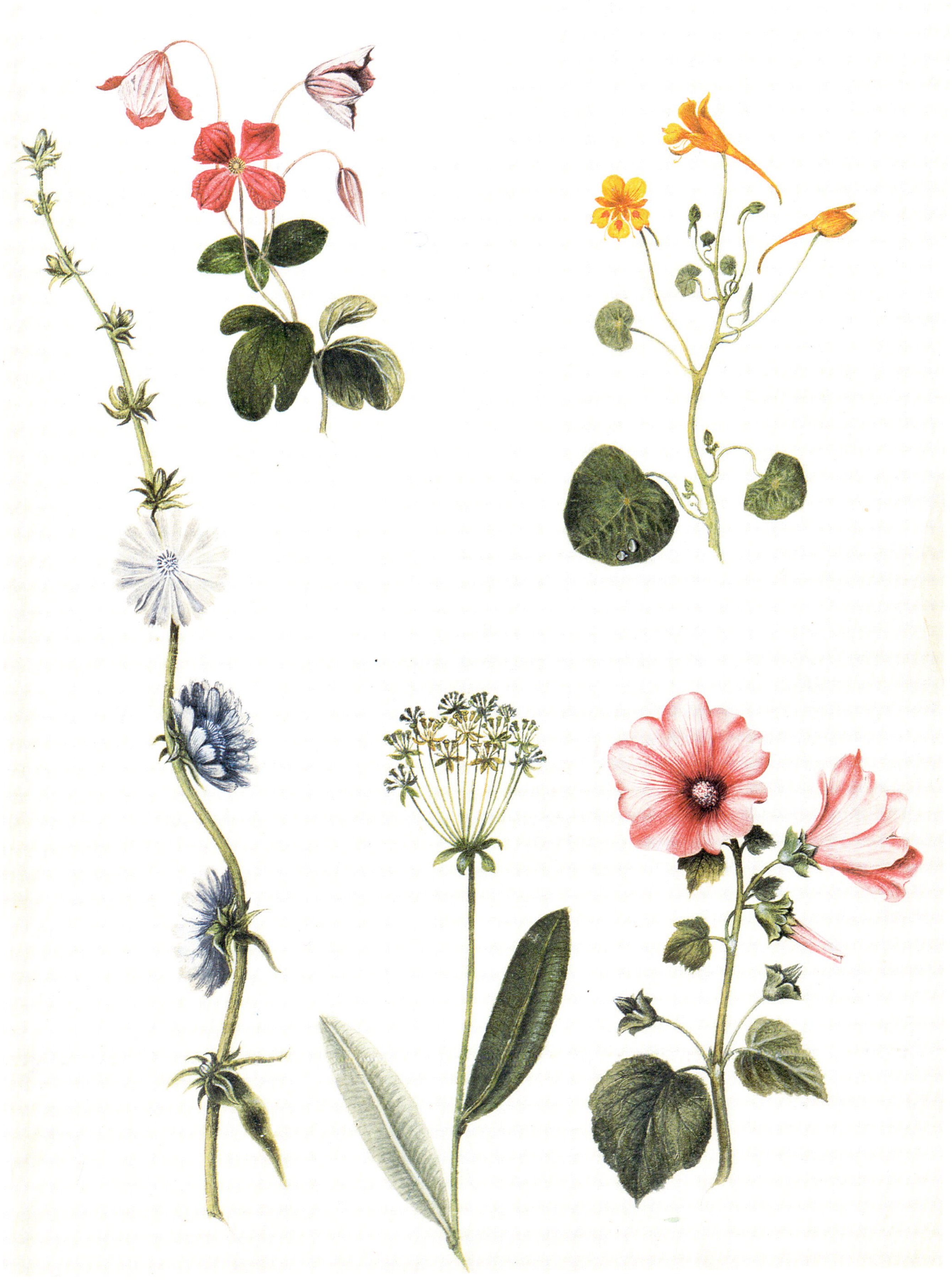

A 'Nasturtium'

The Spanish or Blush Mallow (shown on lower right of page 83) is rather similar to our own Tree Mallow but without the latter's woody stock. It was treated, in gardens, as an annual. The clematis (top left) was then called '*peregrina*' the foreigner – a weak climber, but a fine challenge to Marshal's colour-sense. The umbrella plant shown below is not Cow Parsley as named in the Index to the album but almost certainly a sprig of the shrubby *Bupleurum fruticosum* or Hare's Ear.

Chicory, on the left, was formerly cultivated by farmers as cattle food as well as by gardeners, and by those who wished to adulterate coffee.

Some Carnations

Carnations

Space allows but a small selection of the many carnations that Marshal included in his album. They include varieties named 'La Belle Catherine', 'General Wiggins', the 'Nymphe Royalle', 'The Venetian Imperial Tapisserie', 'General Cornelius', 'Red Admiral of Zealand', 'Le Beau d'Ypres', and 'Huguenot convertie': the last four names showing the continuing horticultural link with the Low Countries.

Our plate shows (clockwise) 'Pasemanack ou picolomey', 'Empereur', 'Amelia d'Orenge', and two unnamed buds. But the titles in this case suggest the French connection. 'Pasemanaque' (for the parti-coloured carnation) indeed throws a sidelight on French influence over the social life of the period. For *passe-manque* were calls used by roulette players who betted that the ball would end up in either one of the slots numbered 19 to 36 (*passe*) or in one of those between 1 and 18 (*manque*).

The game was devised in 1655 by Blaise Pascal, the French mathematician and philosopher, and was taken home by royalist exiles returning to London during the later years of the Commonwealth as a relief from Hazard or Basset.

John Rea, the floriculturalist, whose comprehensive work *Flora Ceres and Pomona* appeared in 1665, listed 91 cultivated varieties of carnation. Thus the plant had come a long way from the days when the Romans used the original Clove Carnation – *Dianthus caryophyllus* – to improve the flavour of their wine.

There seems to be no really convincing explanation for the original of the name 'carnation' which came into use around 1538, as an alternative to the existing Gilliflower or July Flower. Possibly the florists wished to distinguish the *Dianthus* from other July flowers, in particular stocks, for which the same name was used. Carnation may have been a corruption of coronation, the word for a garland, or a shortened form of incarnation, a reference to the flesh colour of the blooms.

The 'pinks' of Shakespeare and others are thought to have referred to the miniature slashes cut in materials to enhance their design or coloration. Flowers with slashed or fringed petals were therefore 'pinks'. Much later, pink became less exclusively botanical and denoted a sign of good health in the cheeks of those said to be 'in the pink'. As a colour in its own right it was first used in 1720.

The blooms shown here are what we would call Border Carnations though they were frequently grown in pots and moved in and out of doors according to their constitution and the weather. They were developed from crosses between the Clove Pink and the Common Pink, *Dianthus plumarius*, the petals of which are slashed almost to the middle.

Both the Clove Pink and the Common Pink were non-native, introduced plants. The Clove Pink still grows wild on the battlements of Rochester Castle, on the outer wall to the left of the main entrance, where it is safe from collectors. Its seeds may well have been brought there by the Normans in their stores. The Common Pink also survives on old castle and abbey walls and occasionally on steep chalky banks.

Marshal, however, did not entirely neglect our truly native pinks. He painted an excellent portrait of the Deptford Pink, *Dianthus armerius*, and listed it as 'Single read Sweet Johns'. This is the delicate pink-flowered species which, as David McClintock has pointed out, has been wrongly so-called over the centuries. John Gerard described a pink that he had seen growing at Deptford. It was however another species, *Dianthus deltoides*, truly a pink, but one with the blush of a Major-General. Yet *D. deltoides* was accepted as the Maiden Pink instead of *Dianthus armerius*. A make-up man had linked the wrong illustration to Gerard's caption.

The illustrations are shown on p.87

The gooseberry below is named the 'Dutch gooseburie, *uva crispa provincialis*', confirming once more that *provincialis* at this time may have referred to the United Provinces. Though the aggrandisement of the gooseberry did not come to pass until the nineteenth century when prize-shows in the working-class districts of the north of England were as keenly contested as those for auriculas and gold-laced polyanthus, the fruit here is of a respectable size, and the flavour of green gooseberries has ever been superior to that of the red, yellow or whitish varieties, ensuring an abundance of visitors to the kitchen garden.

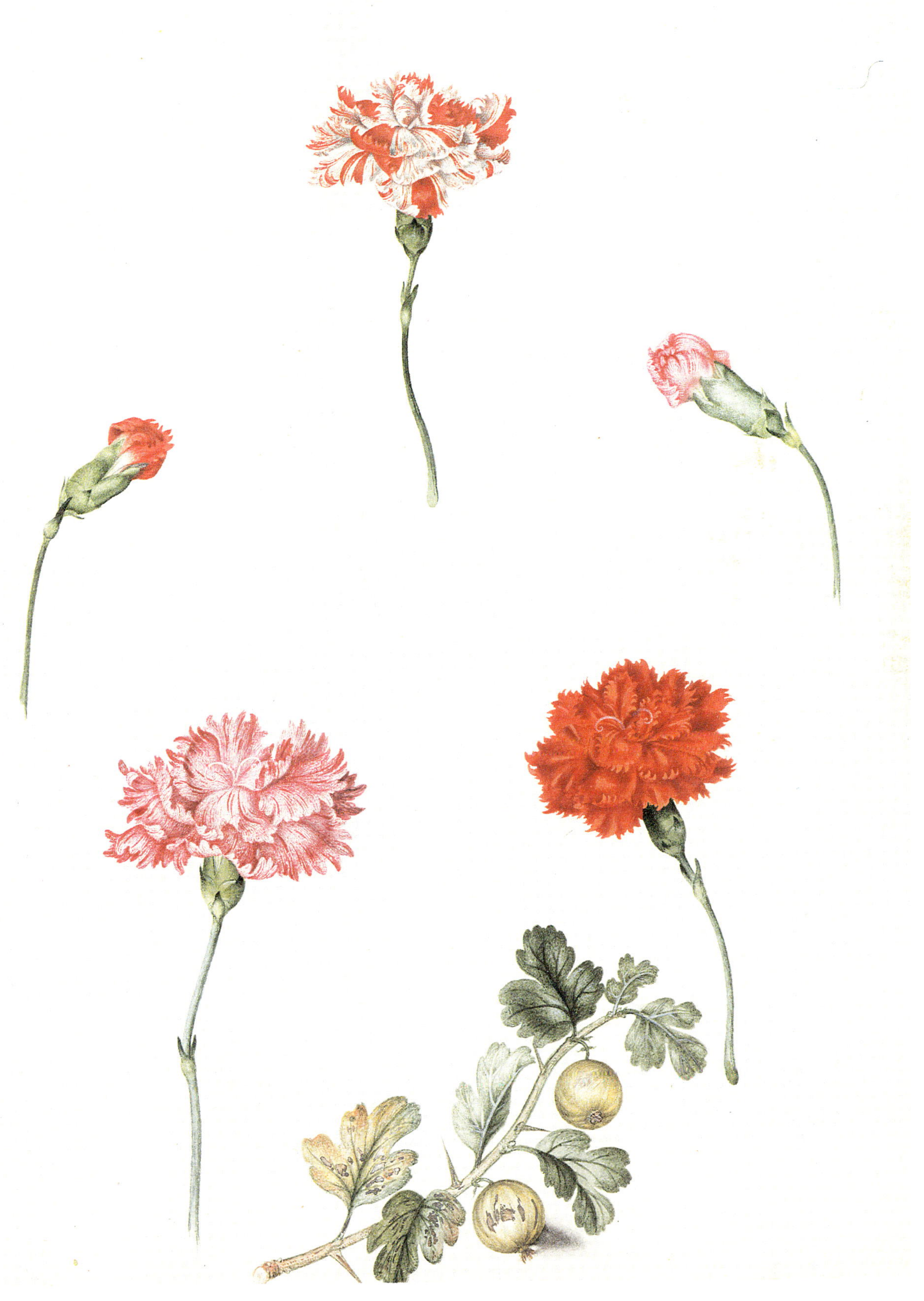

The Fox & Cubs

Mouse Ear or Golden Hawkes Head
Hieracium hortense Latifolium sive pilosella maior
Golden mouse eare, or grimme the Colliar

We should be grateful for the fact that, out of all the highly confusable species of *Hieracium* – at least 260 are recognized in Britain – this Orange Hawkweed, now known as *Hieracium aurantiacum*, should have been chosen by Marshal to decorate the 129th page of his book. For it is highly distinctive and likely to be confounded only with a near relative whose ligules (the strap-shaped projections from each floret) are brownish orange rather than, as in our painting, fiery red.

Both plants are garden escapes, but, curiously enough, Marshal's plant is said to escape more often in Scotland and the north of England, whereas its fellow is seen more often in the south. However, the note on the verso of Marshal's water-colour makes clear that this specimen was a cultivar which had not parachuted over the garden wall or been carried out on a wheelbarrow.

Those unchallenged experts J. G. Dony, F. H. Perring and C. M. Rob stretched a point and included Orange Hawkweed in their standard work *English Names of Wild Flowers* and decided, commendably, to endorse the plant's traditional and distinctive name: Fox and Cubs. But the alternative name, 'Grim the Collier', used with slightly different spelling by Marshal, is still current without any readily apparent explanation. The plant is shallow-rooted and not given to burrowing underground. One might imagine that, like the collie, it got its name from its black hairs – or, more precisely, from the black glands from which they spring. These give both the hairy stalk and the unopened buds a distinctly grimy look. That great Somersetshire plantswoman Margery Fish wrote in her book, *Cottage Garden Flowers*, that she had originally supposed that the name arose from the plant's grim determination, once established, to take over every available inch of space in her beds. But Geoffrey Grigson traces the name back to a play, 'Grim the Collier of Croyden or The Devil and his Dame' by William Haughton who flourished at the end of the sixteenth century, and few will trouble to look further.

The Orange Hawkweed appears at the top of the page opposite

Bramble bush
Rubus
the bramble bushe

Marshal's 'bramble bushe', *Rubus fruticosus*, is no more than a large sprig, but, to the experts of today who recognize nearly 400 different species of blackberry this would be of far greater interest than the more ambitious study made by Leonardo da Vinci of a very much larger branch – a treasure which, like Marshal's water-colour, is preserved in the Royal Library at Windsor.

The large scale on which the portrait is painted makes it just possible to imagine aphids crowding the leaves and bud, but, alas, the 'black' we see is merely oxidized white paint.

The centaury on the right, would, unless it has been painted on a still larger scale, seem to be the Common Centaury, *Centaurium erythraea* rather than 'Centuary, Small, *Centaurium paruum*' as named in the album.

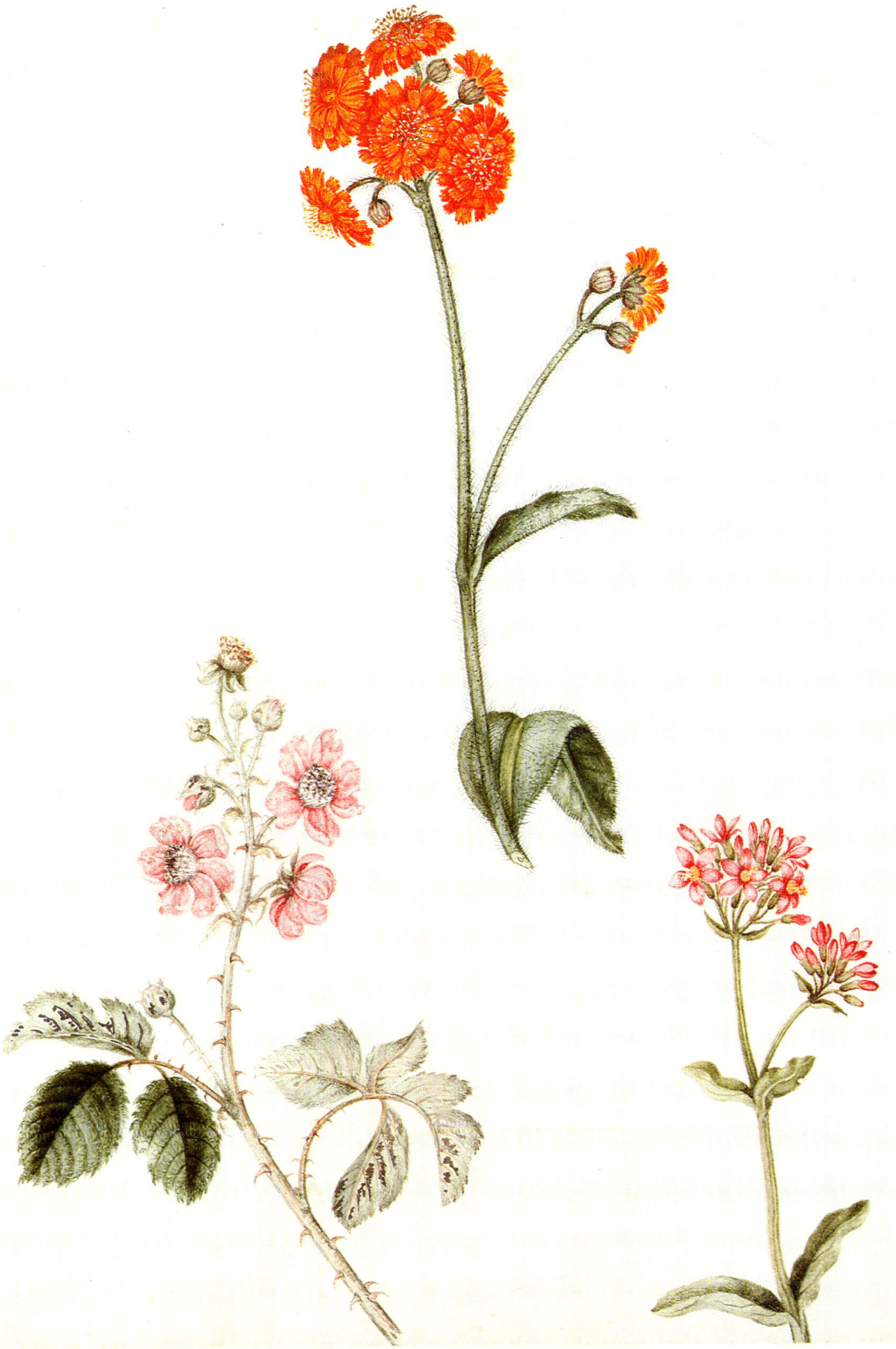

Henbane

Hen, bane black
Hyosiamus Niger
black henbane
Endormie

Here (lower left), Marshal has given us a strikingly beautiful painting of an unloved plant – a portrait which stands out from the page behind as if it were the image of a fashionably dressed woman wearing a polar mink coat, her face slashed with violet lipstick. John Gerard contented himself with saying that: 'The common blacke Henbane hath great and soft stalkes: leaves very broad, soft, and woolly, somewhat iagged, especially thaose that grow neere unto the ground, and those that grow upon the stalke, narrower, smaller, and sharper. The floures are bel fashion of a faint yellowish white and browne within towards the bottome; when the floures are gone, there cometh hard knobby huskes, like small cups or boxes, wherein are small browne seeds.' He might have added that both the veining inside the flowers and the anthers are purple.

Gerard – and Linnaeus – named this species niger or black to distinguish it from a similar plant with whiter, smaller woollier leaves and whiter flowers.

Henbane remains one of those plants which, however attractive it may be in pictures, has never been adopted for the garden. One reason is that it is poisonous and narcotic. It contains Hyoscyamine, a powerful alkaloid obtained from the seeds and used as a sedative – as the French apparently knew when they called it *Endormie,* the sleep-producer. It also contains scopolamine, which, as in the case of its near relative, Deadly Nightshade, can yield a drug used for enlarging the pupil of the eye.

But dangerous drugs alone would not have banned Henbane from becoming a garden plant, for *Colchicum* and Monk's Hood are favourites there to this day. The trouble with Henbane is that it is sticky to the touch and strong-smelling.

Certainly those who wrote about it took no pains to make it desirable. Shakespeare gave these lines to the ghost in *Hamlet*:

Sleeping within my orchard
My custom always of the afternoon,
Upon my secure hour thy uncle stole,
With juice of cursed hebenon in a vial,
And in the porches of my ears did pour
The leperous distilment; whose effect
Holds such an enmity with blood of man
That swift as quicksilver it courses through
The natural gates and alleys of the body . . .

Some scholars have argued that Shakespeare was not referring here to Henbane but to ebony which is black and therefore associated with funerals. But has anyone ever poured a vial of ebony into someone's ear?

John Ray in his *Flora of Cambridgeshire* explored a different medical treatment when he wrote: 'The root of Hyoscyamus placed on coal gives off a smoke with a very unpleasant smell; when pressed through the mouth and nostrils by a tube, it drives out small worms (vermiculi) which sometimes grow in the nostrils or the teeth. They can be caught in a basin of water so that they can be seen better.'

Farmers today are evidently not in this kind of trouble for they do not bother to pull up the plants to get at their roots but content themselves with slashing away at its leaves. It has in consequence become comparatively rare in the wild. It prefers disturbed soil of a chalky nature and is said in consequence to favour rabbit warrens, particularly since rabbits are not partial to the taste.

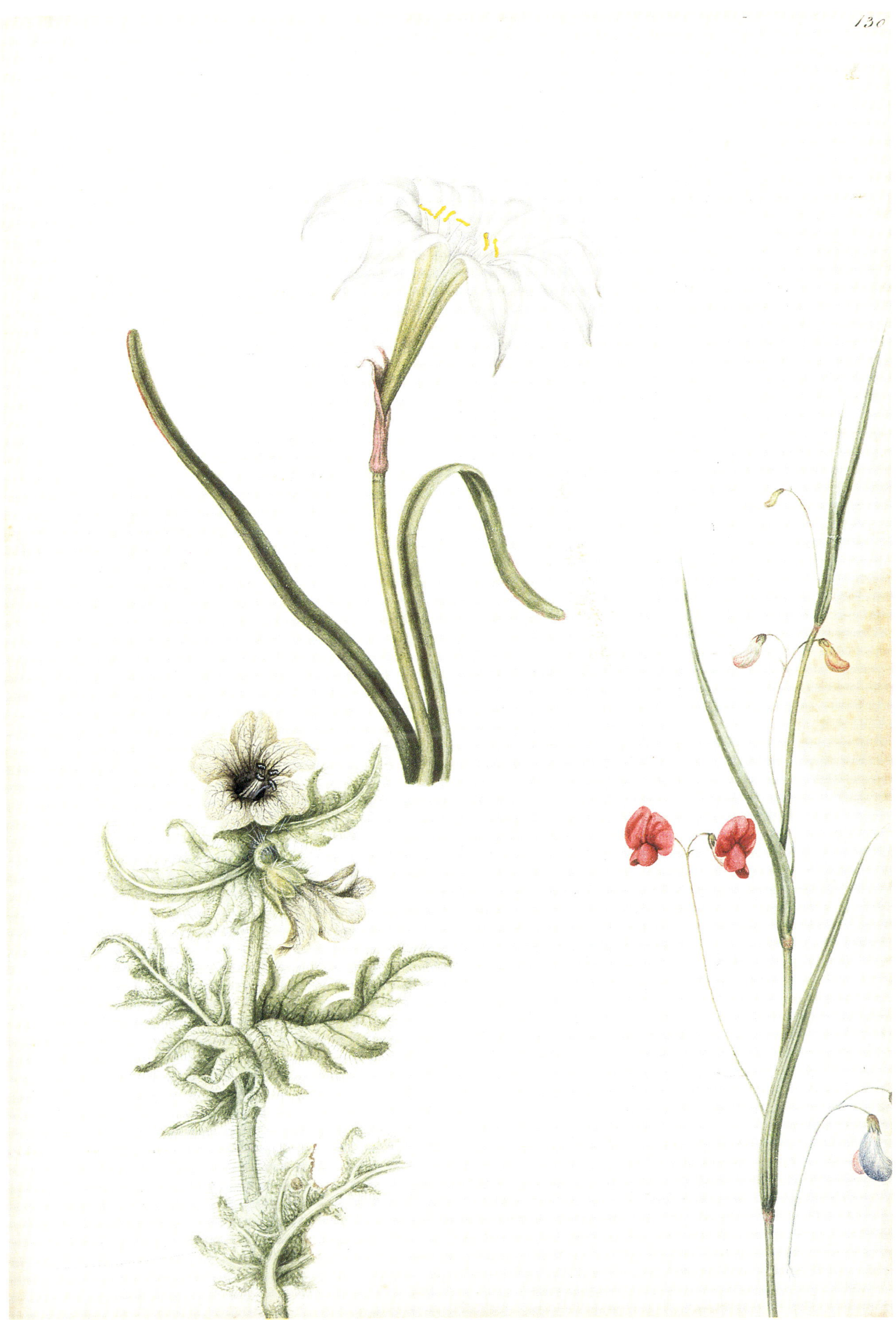

However, its appearances are as erratic as those of *Hamlet's* ghost and are not to be relied on from one year to the next.

A Lily

The lily at the top of page 91 is one of the transatlantic immigrants. Marshal called it 'the Lilie daffodil of Virginia'. We know it as *Zephyranthes atamasco*, the Jamestown Lily, but the first bulbs were probably sent to Tradescant from Paris by Vespasien Robin.

The plant on the right is described as 'Wood Pease or Heath Pease or Crimson Grase Fetch'. It is now *Lathyris nissiola*, the Grass Vetchling, and, on the right day, its flowers glow like rubies in the herbage.

Two Cornfield Flowers

Poppy, single red or Corn Rose–
Papaver rhoeas
Read Popie or Corne Rose

'I have in my hand a small red poppy which I gathered on Whit Sunday on the Palace of the Caesars. It is an intensely simple intensely floral flower. All silk and flame, a scarlet cup, perfectly edged round, seen among the wild grass far away like a burning coal fallen from Heaven's altars. You cannot have a more complete, a more stainless type of flower absolute.'

What Ruskin wrote in prose, Marshal preserved in paint. *Papaver rhoeas*, the Field Poppy, is the most common of our wild species and is far more often seen than *P. dubium*, the Long-headed Poppy, *P. hybridum*, the Rough Poppy, *P. lecoqii*, the Yellow-juiced Poppy, or *P. argemone*, the Prickly Poppy.

According to classical mythologists the poppy was created by Somnus, the God of Sleep, who used it to bring the gift of sleep to Ceres, whose cares were distracting her from bringing on the harvest. Modern farmers, however, believe that it hinders them from bringing in the harvest by taking the goodness out of the land. So it may be that one day the Field Poppy may go the way of the other flowering plants – the cornflower, for instance, and the startlingly beautiful purple decked Field Cow-Wheat, which have been banned by the farmer and are now seldom seen.

According to the very authoritative *Flora of the British Isles* compiled by A. R. Clapham, T. G. Tutin and E. F. Warburg and known colloquially among botanists as 'C.T.W.', the Field Poppy is 'Native or introduced'. It is difficult to be certain which is the case. Like the Corn Marigold, it tends to spring up where the land has been cultivated or disturbed – and nowhere else and in the meantime the seeds can lie dormant for as long as a quarter of a century. Thus it is almost impossible to determine, in any given instance, whether or not a plant has resulted from seed imported through human agency. It grows wild in most of Europe, North Africa, and the temperate belt of Asia, so it might have grown wild here before Britain was cut off from the continent. On the other hand it may have come over the Channel with our earliest farmers – Neolithic man.

The petals of the Field Poppy unlike those of the Yellow Horned-Poppy fall quickly and the flower seldom lasts more than a day.

The flowers contain no nectar, only pollen. But bees like it and scramble round the bottom of the flower, on their sides, in order to get their share. The pollen, however, will not fertilize the ovules of the same plant, so, no matter how much the bees scramble, there is no inbreeding.

Looking once more at Marshal's painting, one cannot help wondering at the way in which the colour has lasted. Marshal, presumably, would not have known about Cadmium Red, a pigment now used by water-colour artists for intense effects but only in commercial production from 1910.

The Two Cornfield Flowers are shown on p.95 top and right

Nigella bastard or cockle
Pseudomelathium
bastard nigella or Cockle

Shown on the lower right of page 95, this plant has been unpopular with farmers because the seeds are large enough to be mistaken for corn, and have been included in the deliveries of unscrupulous seed merchants before the arrival of more sophisticated sorting machinery. We know it as *Agrostemma githago*. 'Cockle' – meaning 'little berry' – is derived from the Latin *coccum*. The plant is one of the Pink family and has no relationship illicit or otherwise with *Nigella* (Love-in-a-Mist) which is one of the buttercups.

Jacob's Ladder

The plant on the left of the page is described as Greekish Valerian, but is, in fact, *Polemonium caeruleum*, Jacob's Ladder. This grows wild in parts of Lancashire and Yorkshire, but is more often seen in gardens as a long-lived perennial. The name comes from the pairs of lateral leaflets here outlined in gold paint which project outwards from the central leaf-rib like the foot-rests of a primitive pole-ladder.

Marshal was unlucky in not being able to show one of the lower leaves of this plant, and we are left in doubt as to whether it was the flower or Marshal's colour that was a little 'overworn'.

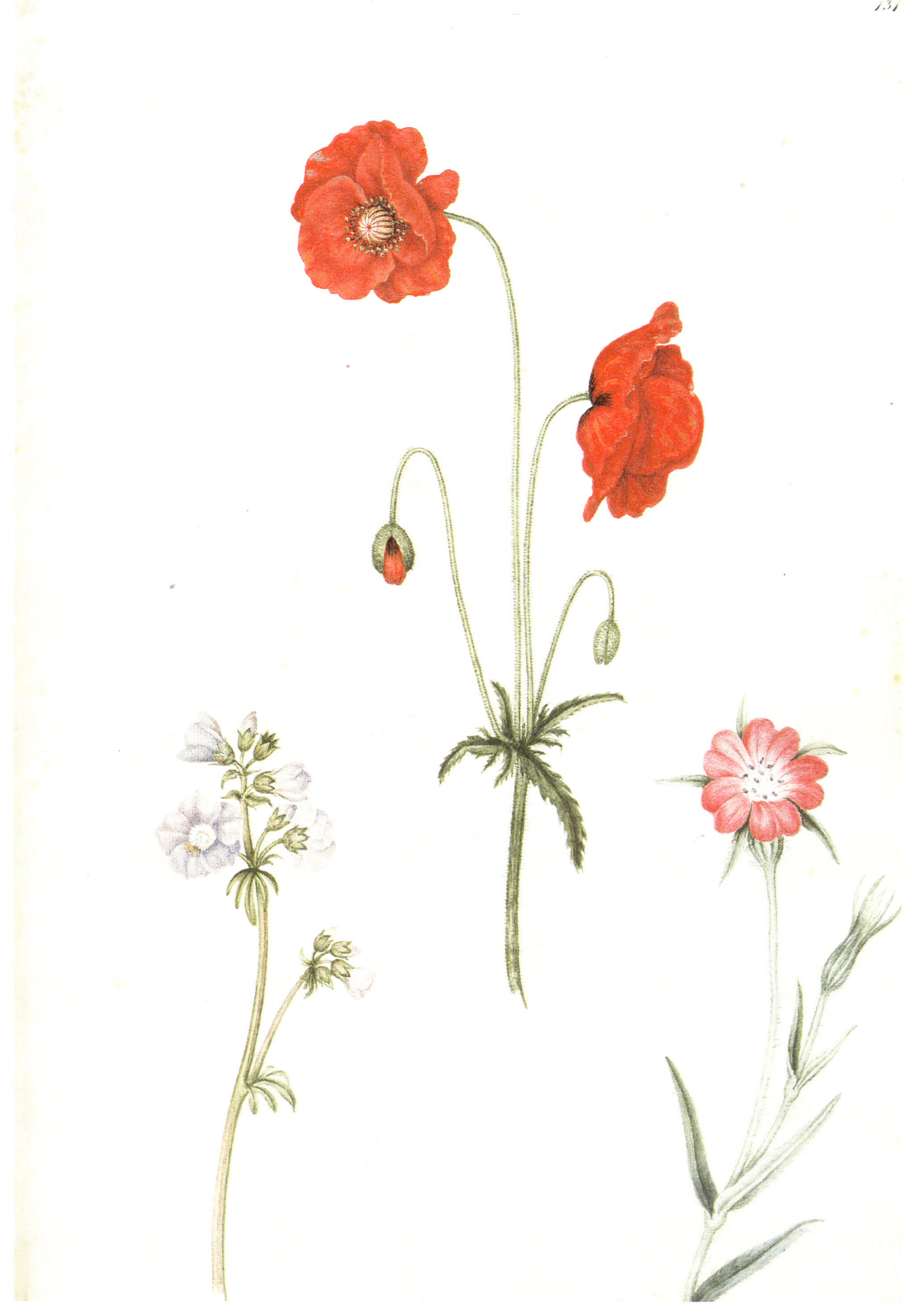
131

Three Marsh Plants: Ragged Robin

Armoraria, ragged robin
Armoraria pratensis mas–
the male Crow flouer or willd william
in french Cuidrelles, or Coucou
Jilieflouer or raged robin

Though the flowers are tattered, the plant is neatly structured, with the flowering branches in pairs about opposite and about equal to each other; the leaves, too, are arranged in pairs. The stamens mature ahead of the ovary which protects the plant from self-pollination.

The Latin name, *Lychnis flos-cuculi*, the Cuckoo Flower, echoes the French description of Ragged Robin and proclaims it as a humble member of the Pink family. It is common in Britain but is a close relative of two very rare plants, the Red Catchfly and the Alpine Catchfly to be found only in two or three remote and inhospitable rockbound localities.

The English for *Cuidrelles* is not to be found in most modern French dictionaries but, according to Godefroi's *Dictionnaire de l'Ancienne Langue Française*, *cuidereau* and its feminine equivalent *cuiderelle* were fifteenth-century words meaning pretentious or presumptuous. But of course it was the plant and not Robin that was feminine.

The Ragged Robin is shown lower right

The Bogbean

Trefoil March
Trifolium palustre Paludosum
march trefoille

Marshal would have risked wet feet had he attempted to paint this plant (shown lower left) *in situ*. For whether in Surrey, Iceland or Morocco, it grows in standing water, both leaves and flowers stemming from beneath the surface. In bud, the flowers are rosy and the petals retain a pinkish tinge on their outer surface. They are decorated within with a whitish fringe. The scape, or leafless stem supporting the flowers, can grow to a foot – all that is needed in sheltered tideless waters.

Though the Bogbean – to use its common English name – is a native plant and by no means unfamiliar to country dwellers, it cannot, at first hand, have been easy to classify. It is in fact a relative of the Gentians but is a maverick in being the only member of its family growing in Britain to have divided leaves. These leaves, or rather leaflets, resemble those of the familiar Broad Bean both in shape and colour; but here the resemblance between the two plants ends. The fruit of the Bogbean is more like a nutlet than a bean and has a point on top; and it tastes extremely bitter.

Though Marshal named this the marsh trefoil, it would be more exact to treat it as a swamp plant. In marshes (and bogs) the summer level of the water is at or near the surface of ground, whereas in swamps the water level in summer remains above ground. But whether in marshes, bogs, swamps, or just ponds, the Bogbean can spread far and wide, making a fine show in early summer. The individual flowers are supposed to last for a month – as might be expected, perhaps, from the lavish supplies of water available to them, and indeed their capacity for

The Bogbean is shown lower left

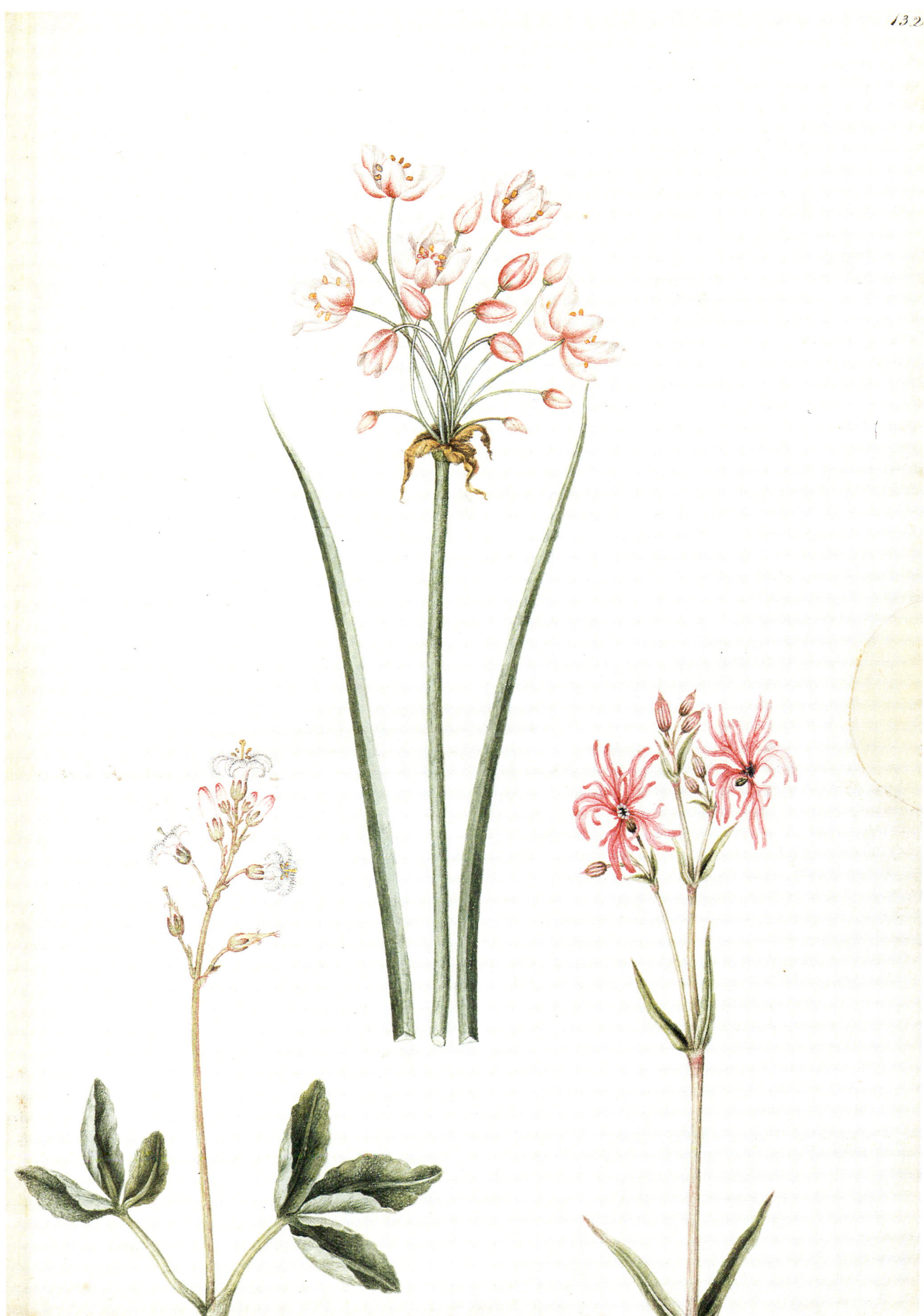
132

survival is commemorated in their Latin name, *Menyanthes trifoliata*, meaning literally Three-leaved Month-flower.

Like the primrose, the Bogbean develops flowers of differing structures. Some have long styles projecting from the flower and in others the style is very much shorter. The supposition is that short-styled flowers can be fertilized only with pollen from long-styled flowers, and vice-versa – thus discouraging inbreeding. Marshal's picture clearly shows that his flowers are of the long-styled type.

Though the Bogbean is still fairly common in Britain, it shares the same threat as other water-plants, that their water supply may become polluted with industrial waste or be drained away altogether by some developer.

The Flowering Rush

Gladiole Water
gladiolus palustris Cordi
Water gladiole

This plant shown in the centre of the page, known to us as the Flowering Rush, *Butomus umbellatus,* is, like the Bogbean, a maverick. It is the only member of the Flowering Rush family *Butomaceae* to be found in Britain, and must have puzzled earlier botanists, who had nothing else with which to compare it. Even the modern name Flowering Rush is not much more accurate than the one that Marshal used. Its leaves are unusual in that, instead of being flat like some at least of the reeds, they are as Marshal shows triangular in section with three sharp edges. This feature earned the plant its botanical name of *Butomus*, coined from two Greek words, which indicate that oxen trying to eat it are likely to get their lips cut. Its attractive cup-like flowers displayed in umbels appear between July and September – rather later than those of the Bogbean.

The Flowering Rush is shown on p.97, top centre

The Flowering Rush is not limited to areas of still water, but can maintain itself in rivers as well as in ponds and ditches, but it is less commonly seen than the Bogbean.

Red Currant

Currant, red
Ribes fructu rubro
read curants

After more than 300 years these currants still remain tempting – someone or some bird has evidently succumbed and eaten a few – and the painting bears witness to the fact that for red and flesh colours Marshal had discovered a technique hardly approached by other artists of his day. It is commendable that he did not paint the bush in April when it would have been in flower, since its blossoms are insignificant and greenish.

Unlike its Black Currant brother, the Red Currant yields no smell from its crushed leaves, a difference which helps to distinguish the two plants in the wild when neither flowers or fruit are showing.

In Marshal's day, the Red Currant was extensively cultivated. Nicholas Culpeper, who was a contemporary of Marshal, and fought in the Civil War, described the fruit in his *Herbal*: 'They are cooling to the stomach, quench thirst and are somewhat restringent; a jelly made with the juice and sugar is cooling and grateful in fevers.'

The Red Currant is shown on p.101, top centre

The Red Flowering Currant which features in so many gardens today was first discovered in the Nootka Sound, off Vancouver Island, in 1792.

Sultan Flower and St John's Wort
Ciannus orientalis
the sultan floeur and Hipericum, St John's Worth

The Sultan Flower was so called because it is said to have pleased 'the great Turke' Suleiman the Magnificent. But this example of it, despite the richly embellished scales of the involucre, would have been summarily rejected by the Supreme Potentate, and even infidels like ourselves would have expected something more akin to the gardener's Sweet Sultan, *Centaurea moschata*, which is endowed with a coronet of rays like those which adorn the Cornflower or the Greater Knapweed. Parkinson, describing the Sultan's Flower said that the rays of encircling leaves [petals] were of a fine delayed purple or blush colour and were 'very beautiful to behold', so we must assume that Marshal was sent a rather poor specimen.

The Sultan Flower is shown on p.101, right

The portrait of the wild St John's Wort is a far better example of Marshal's work. The species, which would appear to be *Hypericum perforatum*, the Common St John's Wort, has been drawn with great attention to detail. The two ridges opposite to one another on the stem are clearly suggested, and it is even possible to detect a hint of the minute glandular dots usually to be seen on the petals of this species.

Marshal apparently found difficulty – not surprisingly – in delineating another distinctive feature of the plant, namely the translucent oil-producing cells which are seen if a leaf is held up to the light. He contented himself with showing a general translucency in two of the leaves. It is reassuring to see that Marshal did not attempt to beautify the damaged stalk, as some earlier painters might have done, but painted it as he saw it.

The plant is apomictic, that is, it is able to short-circuit the normal cell routine and reproduce seed without the formalities of sexual fusion – perhaps because at one time, long ago in its evolutionary history, conditions did not favour the normal insect-induced fertilization.

St John's Wort is shown on p.101, left

The astringent juice which this plant secretes has been greatly prized by the

French, who regard it still as a medicinal plant on a par with the wild rose that yields vitamin-rich hip syrup, and the mallow that promises a cough cure. To them, the Common St John's Wort is *Millepertuis* – the plant with a thousand apertures.

Marshal also painted its better known relative, another wild species: Tutsan, an undershrub whose healing qualities are attested in the French version of its name *Toute-saine*. It is however less generous with its flowers than the species shown here.

The more flamboyant Rose of Sharon, *Hypericum calycinum*, much beloved of park-keepers, was also in the wings. It had been noted by George (later, Sir George) Wheler during his travels to Greece and the Levant in 1675–76, but his own account of his journey was not published till 1682.

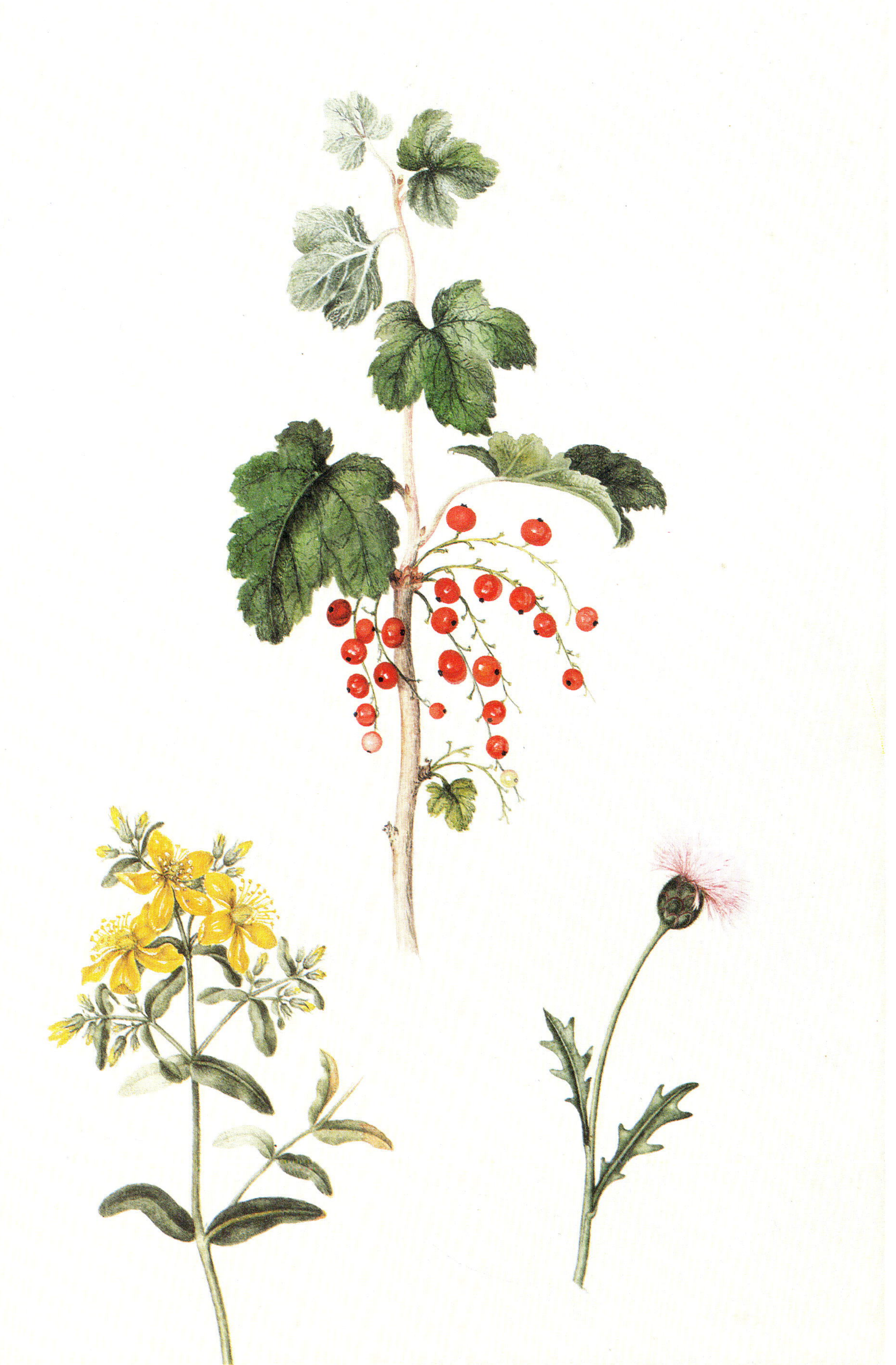

A Sunflower

Sun Flower, female
Flos solis femine
the flower of the sun

Marshal shows, perhaps in fun, a goldfinch supported on one of the leaves of this *Helianthus annus*, waiting for the seeds to ripen.

It will top a nine-foot hedge with flowers 'greater than a great platter or dish' as John Frampton remarked in 1577 and, 300 years later, that argumentative plantsman William Robinson, no friend to other invaders from America, conceded that as an ornamental plant it had much value, 'its robust growth and commanding aspect rendering it suitable for many situations where plants of smaller growth would be quite lost'.

Though Sunflower would seem an obvious name it was earlier known as *Chrysanthemum peruvianum* because it was treasured in that country by sun-worshipping Incas. And the Italians named it *Tromba* (Trumpet) *d'Amore*.

The leaves, which are arranged spirally, are wavy-edged and hairy both above and beneath, but are acceptable to geese and livestock. Bees visit the flowers for nectar and chickens wait beneath for the seeds to fall as from a golden watering-rose on the place beneath.

Rats and mice are very fond of them too, and gardeners are advised that if the flower heads are to be dried for feeding to hens – and there are said to be more than two thousand seeds to a single head – it is best to hang them up safely out of reach of marauders.

Few however will trouble to obtain from the sunflower its most valuable product, oil which is used not only for the salad bowl and the Chinese 'wok' but by some for the paints on the artist's palette.

In olden times the buds were boiled with oil and vinegar and eaten in the same fashion as the tubers of its near relative the Jerusalem Artichoke. These were introduced to England in 1616 in a consignment delivered to John Goodyer, the Hampshire gardener, but, being difficult to peel and prepare, they did not come into favour until the days of Antoine-Augustin Parmentier, who popularized them along with the potato.

Elsewhere on the same page Marshal has drawn a porcupine, a guinea pig, a rabbit and a pair of mallard. He often painted birds and included in his album two partridges, a magpie, a macaw, several green parrots, a heron and a toucan-like bird under which the word 'Onacraterus' is written.

Marshal does not seem to have been deterred by the restlessness of his bird sitters, but in most cases his paintings were on a small scale, with the artist standing a good way from his model. His most successful bird portrait, however, is a close-up on a much larger scale and shows a jay, recently shot and still dripping blood.

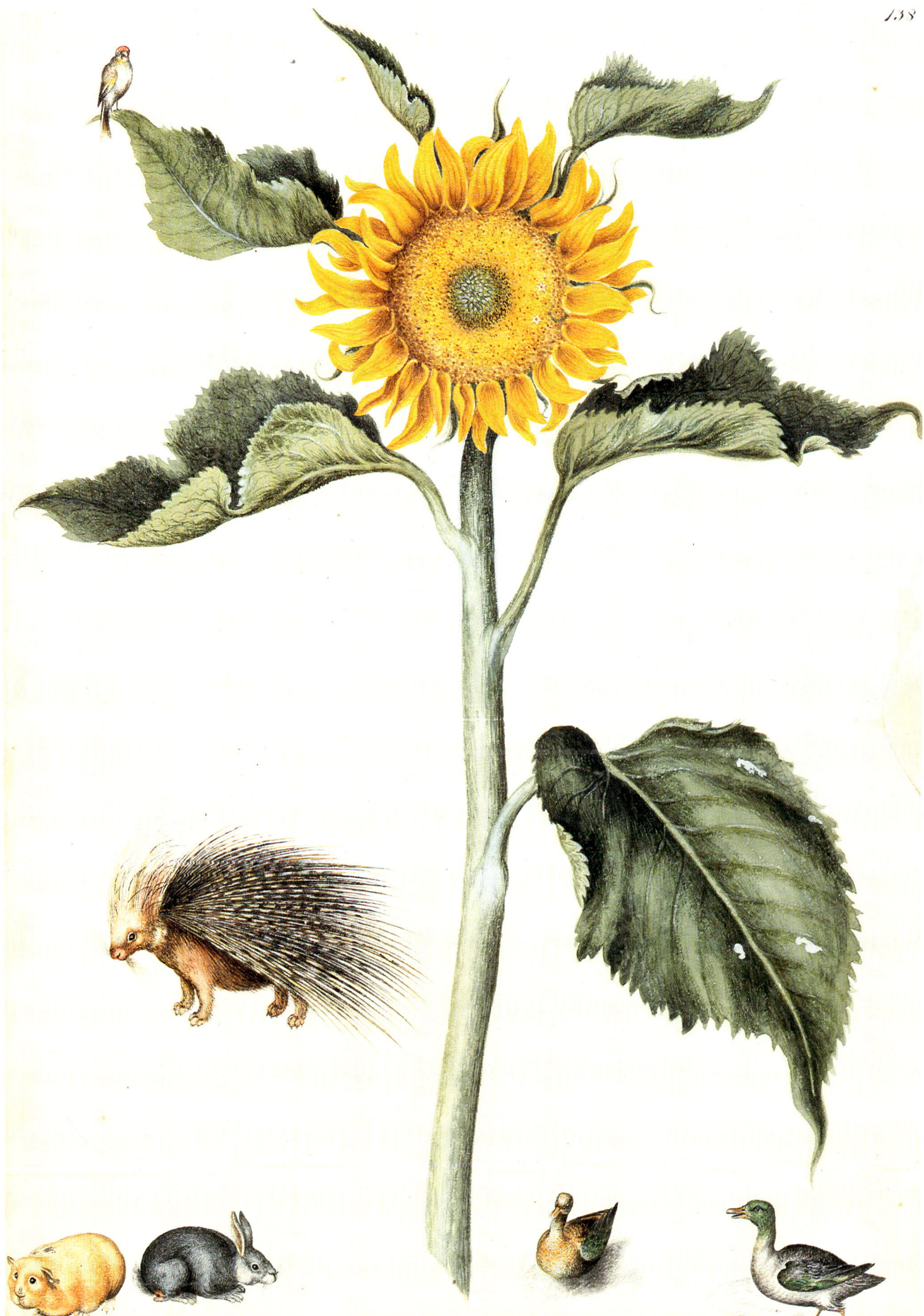
138

The 'Virginian Climber'

Passion Flower
Maracoc sive Clematis Virginiana
The Virginian Climer caled Pasion flouer

A dramatic flower this, and the first which Thomas Johnson added in an Appendix to his new edition (1633) of Gerard's *Herbal.* He said that the Spaniards in the West Indies called it *Granadilla,* because the fruit somewhat resembles a pomegranate. 'The Spanish Friers', he continued, 'for some imaginarie resemblances in the floure, first called it . . . the Passion floure, and in a counterfeit figure, by adding what was wanting, they made it, as it were an Epitome of our Saviours Passion: thus superstitious persons . . . always fashion dreams for themselves.' Devout Catholics saw in the flower's corona the Crown of Thorns, in its five anthers the five wounds suffered by Christ, and in its styles, nails holding him to the Cross.

Johnson described its colour: 'these leaves [petals] are of colour whitish, but thick spotted with a Peach colour, and towards the bottome it hath a ringe of a perfect Peach colour, and above and beneath it a white circle . . .' and adds discouragingly: 'this flower by us is never succeeded by any fruit'.

The 'Virginia Climber' is shown opposite, top right

Johnson names this *Clematis trifolia*, but the white with peach-coloured corona is close to the *Clematis virginiana* described by Parkinson. But Hanmer who called the Passion Flower by the name used by the Indians, Maracoc, said that, apart from the White-and-Peach Maracoc, there was another newer sort of Virginian Maracoc with a yellow flower. Once classified as a clematis, it is today classified in a family of its own, the Passifloraceae.

The flower on the left is described as '*Colchicum neapolitanium fritillaricum* – the Chekerd meadow Safron of Naples', and is the tessellated variety of this plant known today as *Colchicum variopictum.* Two other finely chequered species, *C. agrippinum* and *C. variegatum*, are often preferred today for hybridization.

The '*Planta sensitive* – Sensible plant', shown in a pot, is a close relative of *Mimosa pudica*, the Humble Plant, which John Tradescant Jr had found in Barbados in 1637. The leaves of both these species collapse within seconds if touched, but *M. sensitiva* is less responsive than *M. pudica* and it arrived here ten years later. '*Sensible*', the French equivalent of 'sensitive' would be used without affectation by someone familiar with that language.

Elsewhere on the page: a fairly unremarkable cyclamen leaf described as 'Sow bread leafe'.

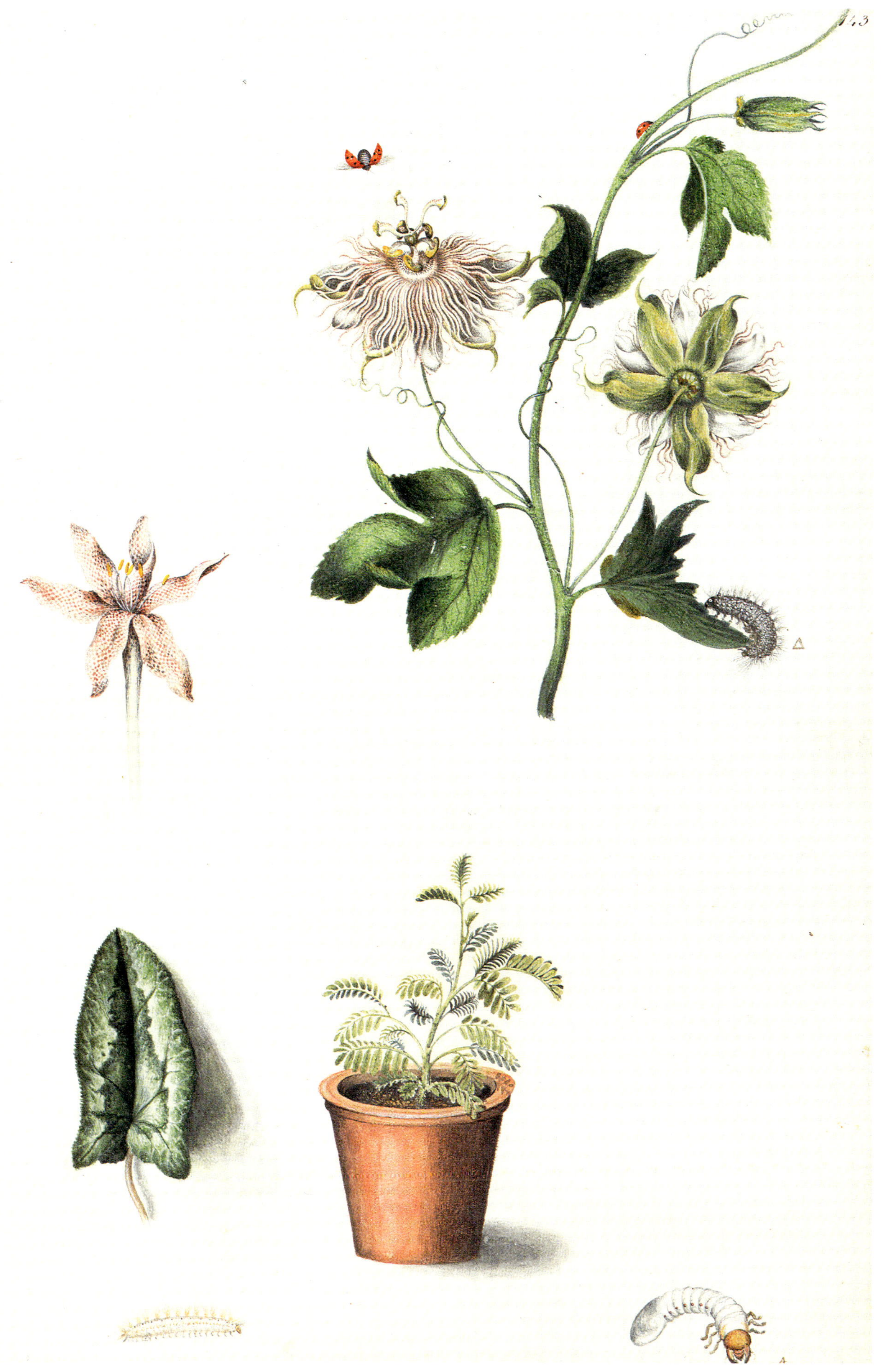

Ginger, Pepper & a Purple-Topped Sage

Ginger as it grew at Fulham
Zinziberis verior Icon
the trew figure of Ginger as it grew at Fulham

The painting by Marshal shows as much of this plant as one might expect to see, for its yellowish green and purple flowers, displayed in dense cone-like spikes, seldom appear in captivity. Commercially it is never sown, but is propagated by division of its rhizomes. It has been a well-known and popular spice in England since the eleventh century.

Zingiber officinale is said to be native to Bengal and Malabar, south-west India, but soon became international; and it is not the only member of its family to have travelled widely. The blander banana, the tough Manila Hemp and the imperious *Strelitzia* belong to the same natural order.

The Ginger Plant is shown opposite, centre

Pepper Guinea
Capsicum Longioribus Siliquis
Long Codded Guinie Peper

Here we see two other members of the nightshade family: two varieties of *Capsicum annuum*. Both are fairly large codded, or podded as we now say, and would therefore be fairly mild in the mouth, for, in general, the smaller the pod, the hotter the taste.

Capsicum and ginger meet together in curry and a traditional Creole recipe combines the two in a pimento paste for which red peppers are chopped and the seeds removed. The pods are then pounded with pestle and mortar together with ginger, onions and salt, and transferred to a well-stopped jar with a layer of best oil on top. Stored in this manner, the paste will keep indefinitely.

Purple-leaved Clarie
Horminum syluestre follis purpureis
clarie with purple leaves

Salvia verticillata, the Whorled Sage, is a species noted for its purple leaves, but the flowers are in whorls of as many as twenty, and the leaves are stalked, so this seems more likely to be *Salvia horminum*. It flowers in rocky places in continental Europe and is usually known as the Red-topped Sage. Its top however is frequently purplish. Marshal mentions the plant's 'purple leaves', but it is the bracts rather than the petals that make the display.

Purple-leaved Clarie is shown opposite, right

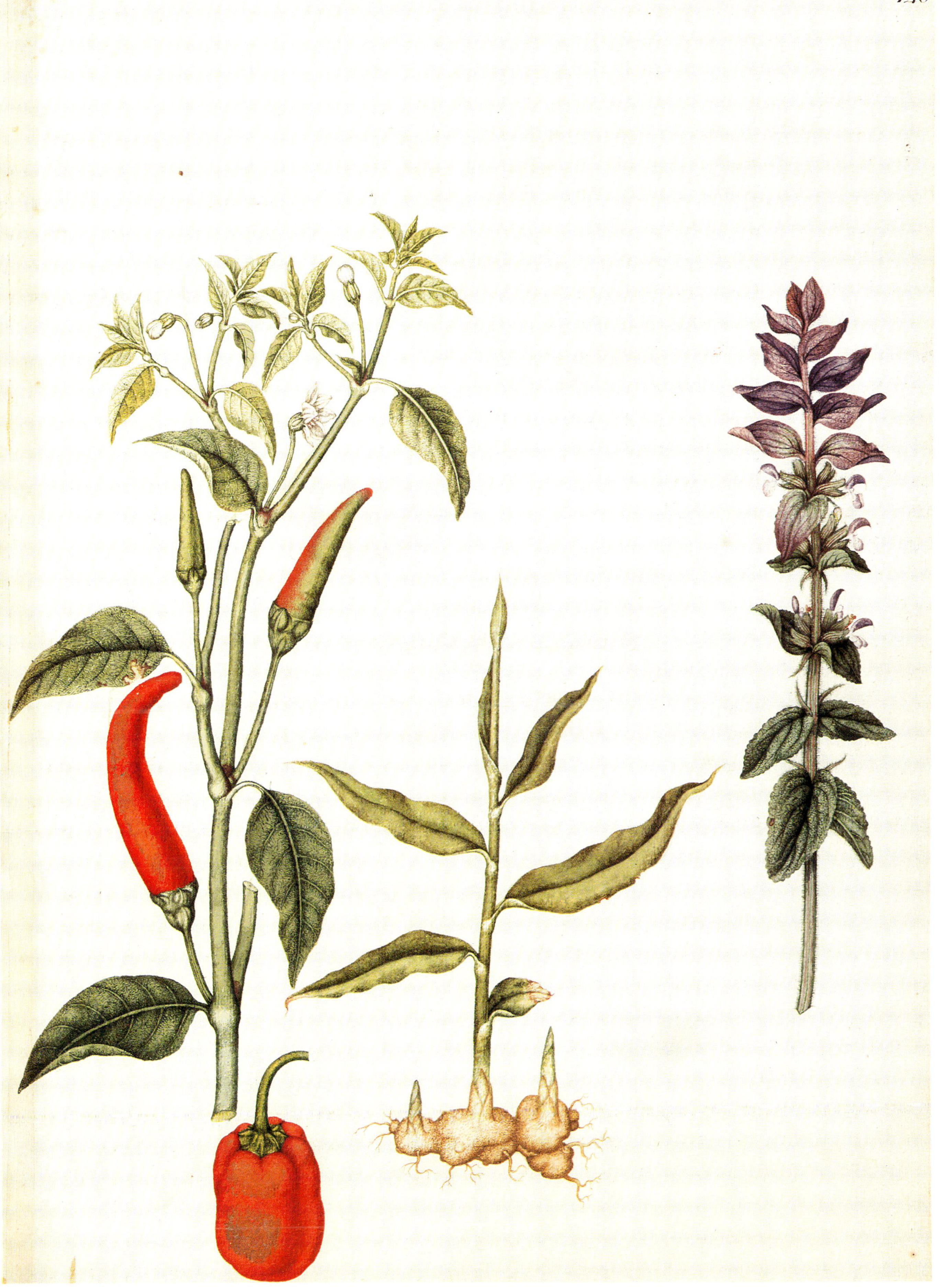

The Guernsey Lily

Lily of Guernsey
This flower was sent me by Generall Lambert August 29th 1659 fro Wimbleton

Samuel Hartlib (d. 1670?), Polish immigrant and friend of Milton, described Marshal as 'one of the greatest Florists' i.e. growers of flowers, who 'deales for all manner of Rootes, Plants and seeds from the Indies and elsewhere'. Hartlib added that Marshal 'blamed' English gardeners for not taking sufficient care to 'preserve and propagate [the] curiosities of flowers which they had gotten'. Yet Marshal was unable to name this wonder-bloom. The name 'Lily of Guernsey' appears in Marshal's album in pencil on the verso of the sheet, in another (later) hand, and again in the index. Marshal the first to paint this flower in Britain made apparently more than one portrait of it, for Dr William Freind lists the portrait of the Guernsey Lily as being among the three sheets missing from the album. He specified that folio 153 'contg a *Guernsey Lilly* . . . was cutt out of a Book by a Lady of great Rank at Chelsea to whom my father had lent it'. Dr Helen Brock, who has made an intensive study of *Nerine sarniensis* surmises that the lady could have been Mary, first Duchess of Beaufort, another great florist, who owned property in Chelsea. Certainly the Duchess thought sufficiently highly of the plant to commission two further portraits: one by Everhadus Kickius the Dutch painter and another by Daniel Frankcom, an under-footman at Badminton who was encouraged by the Duchess to paint flowers. Frankcom's portrait, preserved in *The Book of Flowers* at Badminton, shows two plants, apparently grown indoors, flowering together in a large painted china flower-pot.

General Lambert, having taken up arms for Parliament against the King in 1642 at the start of the Civil War, had become Commander of the Army in the North and later became a Member of Cromwell's Council of State. In May 1652 he had bought the Manor of Wimbledon with its gardens which had been set out by Charles I's Queen Henrietta Maria, in which some of the plants installed by John Tradescant the younger could well have survived. Lambert became well known as a fancier of tulips, and his likeness, holding a tulip, appeared on one of a pack of satirical playing cards (the eight of hearts). Thomas Flatman, poet and miniature painter, lampooned him as Don Juan Lamberto, the Knight of the Golden Tulip. Following a disagreement with Cromwell in 1657 Lambert was expelled from the Council of State and stripped of his honours, and he then retired to his garden. At the time the Guernsey Lily was sent to Marshal on 29th August 1659 Lambert, temporarily back in favour, was helping to suppress a royalist rising in the north-west of England. Presumably Lambert left instructions with his agent at Wimbledon that when the Guernsey Lily flower was at its best, it should be sent to Marshal to record.

There has been considerable speculation as to the early history of the Guernsey Lily. (It is, of course, an amaryllis and not a lily, though the distinction did not become official until Linnaeus's day.) It was originally thought to have come from Japan and, according to Wilfrid Blunt in *The Art of Botanical Illustration*, it appeared in Paris in the garden of Jean Morin in October 1634. An etching of the same plant was included in Jacques Philippe Cornut's *Canadensium Plantarium Historia* (1635) under the title of '*Narciss. Japonicus Rutilo Flore*' (the Japanese Narcissus with the Red Flower). It was not until well on in the eighteenth century that it became clear that *Nerine sarniensis* was a native of Table Mountain on the slopes above Cape Town, not very far from where the Dutch East India Chartered Company had set up their permanent trading station in 1652. Long before this, however, ships from the Far East would be calling in at the Cape for refitting and fresh water, and some confusion about the origins of the plants they brought

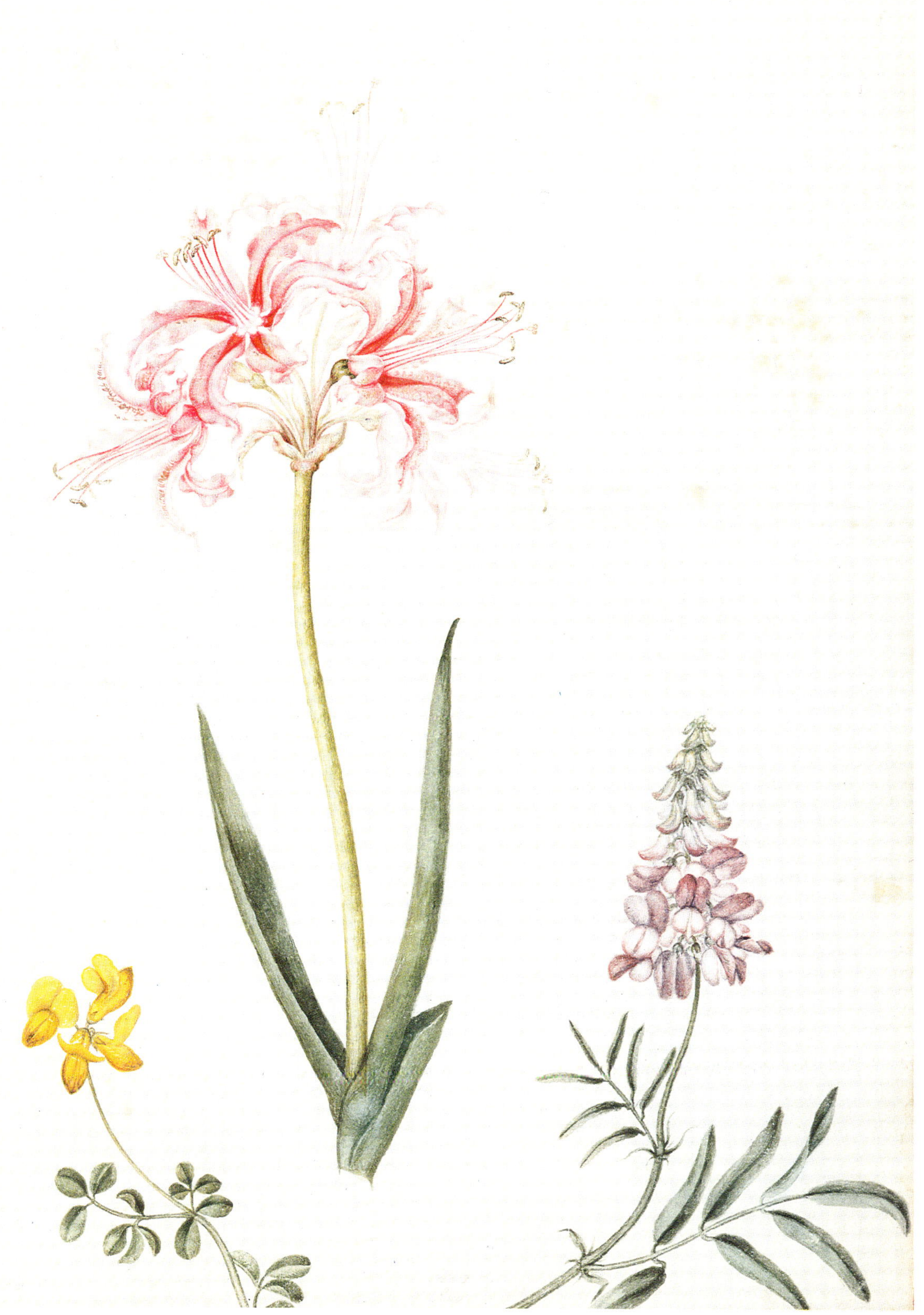

home with them to Europe is understandable. Some of the vessels putting into the Cape would have been French.

How *Nerine sarniensis* reached Guernsey is another matter of speculation. James Douglas, whose work *Description of the Guernsey lilly* was published in 1725, was greatly impressed with the story put about by the botanist Robert Morison (1620–83) and subsequently discredited, according to which the lily bulbs growing in Guernsey had been cast up there from a shipwreck. Morison's source was probably another botanist Charles Hatton (1635–c. 1705), younger son of the first Baron Hatton, Governor of Guernsey.

An alternative explanation, also considered by Douglas, came from Henry de Sausmarez, who said that his grandfather, Jean de Sausmarez, was the first person in Guernsey to receive the bulbs which were given him as a present sometime during the 1640s. Jean de Sausmarez (b. 1609) was made Jurat of the Royal Court in 1653 and as such he served in the Admiralty Court which dealt with claims for payment for servicing damaged ships of various nations. He would thus have been well placed to meet shipwrecked sailors and passengers – more so, perhaps, than during the 1640s. The plant could have already reached England at or before the mid-1650s according to a note in *The Garden Book* of Sir Thomas Hanmer. Referring to an amaryllis bulb from Barbados which had been sent to him by a friend, Sir Thomas wrote: 'Three rootes of this kind bore that yeare [1655] in three several gardens in and neere London, but never since, though some of them are yet living, anno 1659, but different from what they did the first yeare, they did put their greene leaves forth of the earth in May, and kept them all the sommer, but no signe of stalk or flowers. I guesse this to bee an Autumnal bulbe, which bore with us out of its season upon transportment from the West Indyes hither, being out of the earth when the leaves should have come forth, and it is usual for bulbes that come from remote parts to beare the first yeare and not afterwards, though the rootes live still, as I have seene often the experience of the flower of Garnsey as we call it.'

If, after all, Henry de Sausmarez was correct in giving the 1640s as the arrival date for the first bulbs of the Guernsey Lily, then a ready, though admittedly speculative, explanation is forthcoming as to who would have sent them to this country. Henry Danvers, Earl of Danby, was a fervid horticulturalist, who established the Botanic Garden at Oxford. He was Governor of Guernsey for 23 years (from 1621 till his death in 1644). He could have sent over the first consignments of bulbs, and, though others may have followed, the English gardeners, blamed by Marshal for their incompetence had little or no success – even in the Botanic Garden at Oxford – until Lambert's magnificent flower appeared.

The unravelling of the history of the Guernsey Lily is not helped by the fact that Lambert, who had been sent in battle order to oppose the Restoration and in consequence was imprisoned for a time in the Tower of London, was afterwards exiled to Guernsey.

Trefoil, small codded
Trifolium Selinquosum minus
Small Codded trefoille

Despite the description 'small codded' the plant looks like *Lotus corniculatus*, called Birds-foot Trefoil because the seed-pods (some 3 centimetres in length) when ripe are set like the claws of a bird's foot. The larger codded trefoil could have been *Tetragonolobus maritimus*, 'Dragons Teeth', a true trefoil which was formerly *Lotus siliquosus*.

The Small Codded Trefoil is shown on p.109, bottom left

Rue Goats, Purple
Galega
goats Rew

This plant with its faded pea-blossoms has little merit in the garden. It bears the name *Galega officinalis*, but Culpeper declared, 'This plant is seldom used in the shops.' He nevertheless recommended it as 'good against pestilentious distempers' and for sweating out fevers.

Goat's Rue is shown on p.109, bottom right

The Chinese Lantern

Cherry Winter
Solanum vesicarium sive Alkakengi
Winter Cheries

Known to some unaccountably as the Cape Gooseberry, the Winter Cherry (*Physalis alkekengi*) belongs to the invaluable nightshade tribe which has provided us with the egg-plant, the tomato and the potato. Its own fruit, however, though edible, is not highly esteemed.

The Chinese Lantern Plant – the most logical name for this garden favourite – is spread widely across the temperate zone from the Caucasus to the Far East. It shows white flowers in July and August, and, when these drop, the calyces develop into the bright red, papery lanterns. In the open, the paper rots, leaving only a loofah-style open network around the fruit; but, if brought in early and dried, the lanterns do much to enliven the winter flower-bowl.

Though there were earlier references in Britain to 'Alken Kengy' it was William Turner, the Elizabethan botanist, who first mentioned and described the Winter Cherry as growing in Britain. The name appears in a list which he prepared in 1548 of plants growing in England. John Gerard mentioned the plant in his *Herbal* published in 1597 and showed a woodcut of it taken probably from an earlier work. An illustration of a similar plant appears in the *Codex Vindobonensis* which was prepared in about AD 512 to illustrate Dioscorides' earlier work *De Materia Medica*.

The Chinese Lantern Plant is shown opposite, lower left and its fruit on the right

The name 'Alkekengi' is thought to have had an Arabic origin.

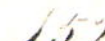
152

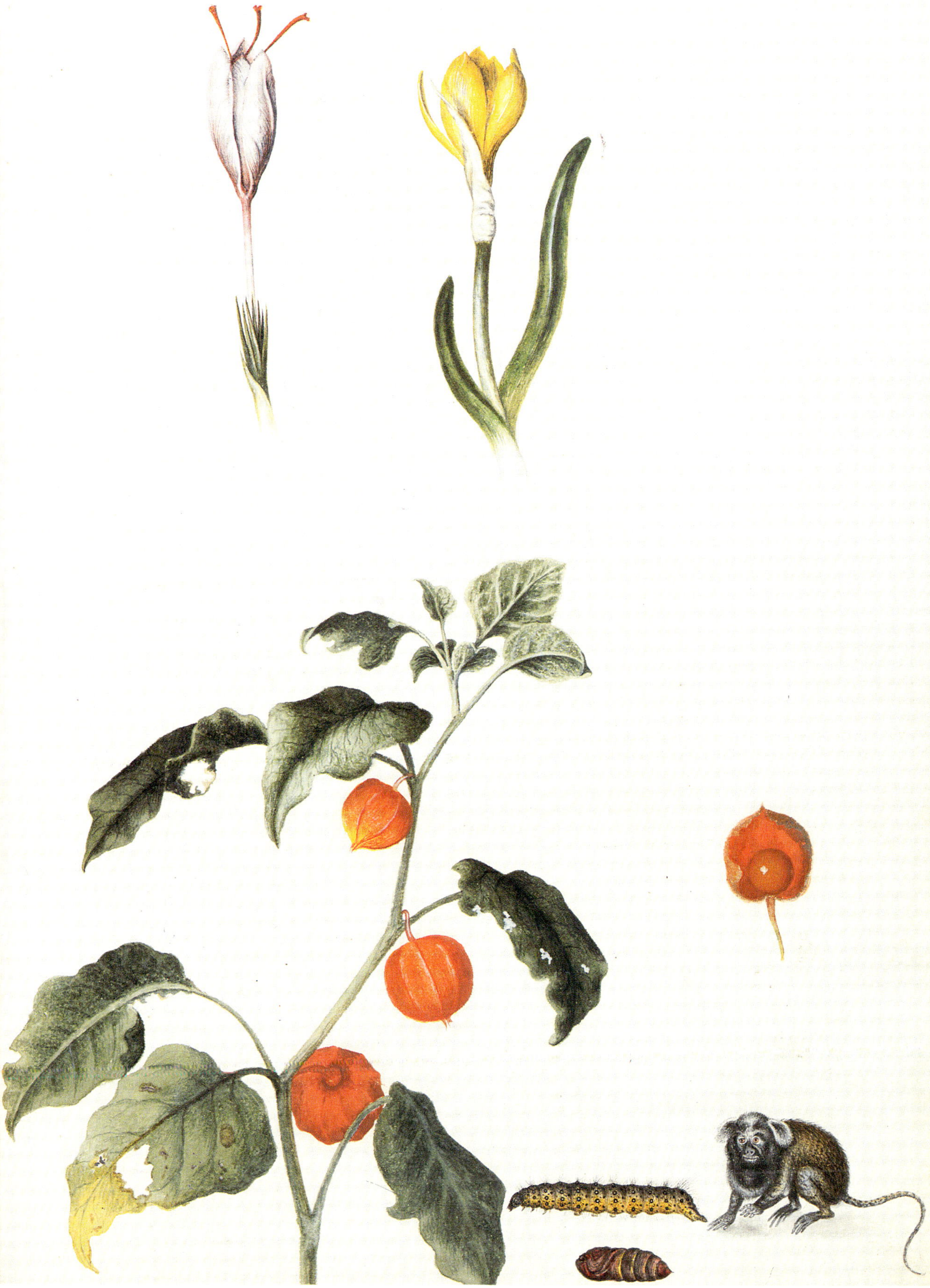

The True Saffron

Crocus, true saffron
Crocus verus Salinus autumnalis
The trew safron

The True Saffron, *Crocus sativus*, provides the spicy flavouring to be relished in bouillabaisse and the primrose-coloured rice dishes of the Mediterranean. It has even been used in Britain to enliven sponge-cake and bread. The flavour is derived from the stigmas of the flowers and it has been calculated, on a small sample, one supposes, that some 150,000 stigmas with the style attached, are needed to provide a kilogramme of the dried spice.

The labour involved in preparing the condiment has kept the price high and the temptation to adulterate the product with something less costly became so great that in mediaeval times the penalty for doing so was death.

The True Saffron is not easily grown, but the gardeners of Saffron Walden in Essex certainly had the knack, and three crocuses were incorporated in the town coat-of-arms. According to a local legend the first saffron corms to reach Saffron Walden were smuggled there in the hollowed staff of a pilgrim returning from the Holy Land.

The True Saffron is to be sharply distinguished from the so-called Meadow Saffron, *Colchicum autumnale*, which also flowers in the autumn.

Colchicum is highly poisonous, but can be distinguished without difficulty from the True Saffron. Being a member of the lily family, it has six stamens to each of its flowers. The crocus, being a member of the iris family has, as Marshal unhesitatingly shows, but three.

The True Saffron is shown on p.113, top left

On the right of the True Saffron is a flower described as 'The Great Autumne or Winter Dafodil'. At first sight it might be taken for a crocus. But the leaves are not tufted and no really yellow crocuses are to be found in autumn and winter (unless you count February). So this must be a *Sternbergia* – probably *S. clusiana* which is the larger of the two best-known species. This flowers from September to November showing brilliant yellow flowers.

The 'Mexcico munky' shown in the lower right-hand corner could not have been the easiest of sitters.

Willow-Herb

Willow flower, wild filius ante patrem or Lisimachia campestris
Willd willow herbe

The names given to the flower in Marshal's portrait are a part of botanical history. In his time herbs were herbs and flowers were something different. The plant in question had no medicinal virtues, so it could not be a herb. It must be a flower. And it must be a wild willow flower because there was another willow flower which was grown in some gardens. This was Rosebay Willowherb, *Epilobium angustifolium*, of which Parkinson wrote: 'Wee have not knowne where this Willowe flower groweth naturally, but we have it standing in an out corner of our Gardens to fill up the number of delightful flowers.' Today, however delightful it may look, it is considered to be a wild plant.

What added to the confusion was that some other plants such as Yellow Loosestrife belonging to the Primrose family, which is quite distinct from the Willowherb family, were then, as now, also called *Lisimachia* and were said to be 'Willowherbes'.

But, to return to the flower before us: It is the one which Gerard at the beginning of the seventeenth century knew as *Lysimachia campestris* – though in contrary fashion he gave it the name of Wilde Willow-herbe, describing it as follows: 'The wilde Willow-herbe hath frail and very brittle stalks, slender probably about the height of a cubit [roughly 18 to 22 inches corresponding to the length of a man's forearm], and sometimes higher; whereupon doe grow sharp pointed leaves, somewhat snipt about the edges, and set together by couples. There come forth at the first, long slender coddes wherein is contained seed, wrapped in a cottony or downy wooll, which is carried away when the seed is ripe; at the end of which cometh forth a small floure of a purplish colour; whereupon it was called Filius ante Patrem, because the floure doth not appeare until the cod be filled with his seed.'

The general description, particularly the mention of brittle stems, would point to the plant we now know as *Epilobium roseum*, generally known as Pale Willowherb or Small-flowered Willowherb – another feature which accords with Gerard's description.

When closely examined, the stem is seen to have two distinctly raised lines and two indistinct ones. The upper part of the stem is covered with curling white hairs and some glandular ones as well. The seeds bear a plume of long hairs which allows them to be carried by the wind for long distances.

Willow Herb is shown on p.117, bottom right

Today in Britain the plant is widespread but few and far between. It favours waste places, especially damp ones, of which there would have been plenty around London in Marshal's time, and river banks.

Solomon's Seal

The impressive stem to be seen at the top of the page is '*Cigelle Salamonis Virginiana Latifolium*' i.e. the Broad-leaved Virginian Solomon's Seal. Broad-leaved it is, but not so different from two of our native species. One of these, however, Angular Solomon's Seal, *Polygonatum odoratum*, has its flowers singly or in pairs, and the flowers of the other species Common Solomon's Seal are 'waisted' in mid-tube.

Ivy-Leaved Toadflax

The plant on the left, *Cymbalaria muralis*, the Ivy-leaved Toadflax, familiar today on almost every suitable wall, did not apparently arrive in this country before the seventeenth century. It was first reported from William Coys' garden, at North Ockenden in Essex, in 1617.

This little plant differs in one important respect from the larger toadflaxes and snapdragons. These have what is known to botanists as self-incompatibility – a factor which inhibits the fertilisation of the ovules of one flower by pollen from the same flower. The Ivy-leaved Toadflax has no such inhibitions, and the flowers are regularly self fertilised. This inbreeding does not appear to have debilitated the species in any way. As the seeds begin to form, the flowers turn inwards towards the supporting wall, adding to the chances that one of them will drop its seed into a suitable crevice.

Marshal has shown the 'upper' part of the plant with alternate leaves. Those nearer to the root are placed opposite one another, and suggest with greater plausibility the pair of cymbals implied by the Latin name.

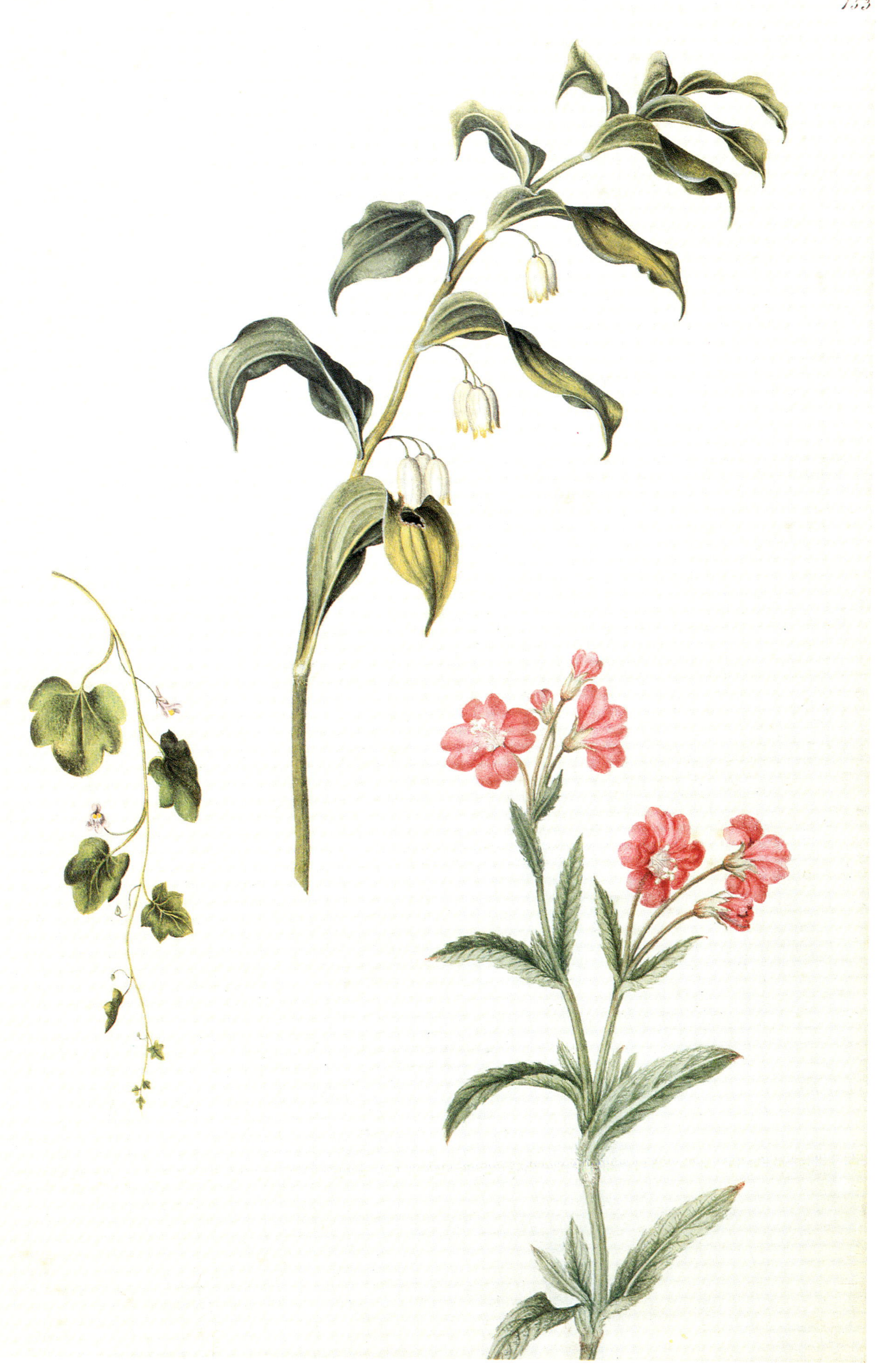

Select Bibliography

Thomas Birch, *The History of the Royal Society of London*, printed for A. Millar in the Strand, London, 1756.

Wilfrid Blunt, *The Art of Botanical Illustration*, London, 1950. *Tulipomania*, London, 1950.

M. E. Bradshaw (ed.), *The Natural History of Upper Teesdale*, Durham County Conservation Trust, 1976.

Edward A. Bunyard, *Old Garden Roses*, London, 1936.

A. R. Clapham, T. G. Tutin, E. T. Warburg, *Flora of the British Isles*, Cambridge, 1962.

Alice M. Coats, *Flowers and their Histories*, London, 1968. *The Plant Hunters*, New York, 1969. *The Treasury of Flowers*, London, 1975.

Peter Coats, *Flowers*, London, 1970.

Gloria Cottesloe and Doris Hunt, *The Duchess of Beaufort's Flowers*, Exeter, 1983.

E. Croft-Murray and Paul Hulton, *Catalogue of British Drawings in the British Museum*, vol. I (*16th-17th centuries*), London, 1960.

Nicholas Culpeper, *Complete Herbal*, 1653 (Reprint, London, 1952).

Charles de l'Ecluse, *Rariorum aliquot Stirpium per Pannoniam Austriam et vicinus quasdam Provincias observatorum Historia*, 1583.

J. G. Dony, F. H. Perring, C. M. Rob, *English Names of Wild Plants*, London, 1980.

Ivy Elstob (ed.), *The Garden Book of Sir Thomas Hanmer*, London, 1933.

Margery Fish, *Cottage Garden Flowers*, London, 1980.

Roy Genders, *Collecting Antique Plants*, London, 1971.

John Gerard, *The Herbal or General Historie of Plants*, 1633, Reprint, New York, 1975.

Geoffrey Grigson, *A Dictionary of English Plant Names*, Harmondsworth, 1973.

Miles Hadfield, *A History of British Gardening*, London, 1979.

Roger Heim (ed.), *Tournefort*, Paris, 1957.

F. Arnold Lees, *The Vegetation of Craven in Wharfedale* (Reprinted from *The North Western Naturalist*, 1937–39; ed. by A. A. Dallman).

Prudence Leith-Ross, 'A Little-Known Botanical Artist: Alexander Marshal' *Apollo*, Feb. 1984, pp. 104–7.

David McClintock, *Companion to Flowers*, London, 1966.

David McClintock and R. S. R. Fitter, *Collins Pocket Guide to Wild Flowers*, London, 1974.

Oxford Botanical Garden, *Catalogue of Plants Grown*, 1659.

John Parkinson, *Paradisi in Sole Paradisus Terrestris*, 1629 (Reprint, London, 1904).

Michael Proctor and Peter Yeo, *The Pollination of Flowers*, London, 1979.

John Ray, *The Flora of Cambridgeshire* (translated from the Latin by A. H. Ewen and C. T. Prime), Hitchin, 1975.

Readers Digest, Encylopaedia of Garden Plants and Flowers, London, 1979.

Florence White, *The Good Things of England*, London, 1936.

Unpublished Material

Helen Brock, Researches into the name, place of origin, and appearance in Europe and particularly Guernsey of *Nerine sarniensis*, the Guernsey Lily.

Bibliography for the Preface

W. Blunt, *Tulipomania*, London, 1950 (reproducing 16 of Marshal's watercolours of tulips from the Windsor *Florilegium*).

E. Croft-Murray and P. Hulton, *Catalogue of British Drawings in the British Museum*, vol. I, London, 1960, pp. 440–446.

P. I. Edwards, 'Alexander Marshal . . . Flower Painter', *Proceedings of the Botanical Society of the British Isles*, 5 (3), 1964, p. 230.

R. D. Harley, *Artists' Pigments, c. 1600–1835*, 2nd ed., London, 1982, pp. 34–35 and 112.

P. Leith-Ross, *The John Tradescants*, London, 1984, p. 157.

P. Leith-Ross, 'Two Notes on the Tradescants. I: An Early Clematis Identified. II: Alexander Marshal and "Tradescant's Orchard"', *Journal of Garden History*, vol. 4, no. 2, 1984, pp. 157–161.

P. Leith-Ross, 'A Little-Known Botanical Artist: Alexander Marshal', *Apollo*, Feb. 1984, pp. 104–7.

B. Long, *British Miniaturists*, London, 1929, p. 289.

G. W. Marshall, *Miscellanea Marescalliana*, 1883–88, vol. I, Appendix, pp. 29–30.

J. Mears, 'An Analysis of Information preserved in a recently identified collection of Insect Drawings by Alexander Marshall', *History in the Service of Systematics*, London, 1981, pp. 87–94.

A. P. Oppé, *English Drawings – Stuart and Georgian Periods – in the Collection of His Majesty The King at Windsor Castle,* London, 1950, no. 432.

Vertue Notebooks : The Walpole Society, xviii, *Vertue I*, 1929–30, p. 134.
Hugh Walpole, *Anecdotes*, 1862, ii, pp. 421, 536.

Appendix A

A Note on the Paper and Binding of the Flower Album

The two volumes which now contain Marshal's *Florilegium* each measure 47 × 35.5 cms. Numbers 1 to 79 of the modern foliation are in volume I, and 80 to 159 are in Volume II. Each volume contains preliminary remarks concerning its provenance, and an index. There are traces of an old foliation (as given in Freind's catalogue) on the top right corner of several of the sheets, e.g. ff. 1, 2, 83, 84, 87, 90, 91, 97 (Freind's ff. 1, 2, 85, 86, 93, 94 and 100), indicating that the pages must have been quite substantially trimmed at the time that the new volumes were made up. The individual sheets are guarded into the binding, and several have fragments containing other watercolour studies (of birds, fish, etc.) pasted onto blank areas. During the rebinding process some of these fragments were removed from their former host pages, and are now laid down in a group on f. 158. Many of the sheets have old paper patches slightly below the centre on the outer edge, to replace paper damaged by an oil stain. The fact that the stains (and patches) do not in any way align with each other, and that unstained pages are interspersed with badly stained ones, indicates that the sheets were once kept in a quite different order from today's. Most of the sheets have a horizontal fold roughly across the centre. The absence of paint along the central fold on a few sheets (e.g. f. 83) might indicate that the paper was kept folded even after it had been used by Marshal.

Apart from the early nineteenth-century sheets used for the preliminary pages, and the last pages of volume II, five different types of paper can be distinguished (see Appendix B). It is likely that most, if not all, of these were continental imports. Four of the paper types are cream-coloured. These types are found scattered throughout the two volumes in no particularly logical pattern. Folios 155 and 156 are two paintings on blue paper, as were two of the leaves listed by Freind (but now missing). In addition there are six small sheets of vellum (with paintings of cherries, nuts, oysters, etc.) pasted onto ff. 157–159. These appear once to have been independent works, suitable for framing.

Appendix B

The Freind Catalogue

(British Museum, Department of Prints and Drawings, R 4 3)

Key:

A Heawood 172–174
B Heawood 1372
C cf. Heawood 2289
D Heawood 1765
E Blue paper
F Vellum
? Paper without watermark

f.129 Volume H.I.
Florilegium Alexandri Marshall

This Book was the Work of a Gentleman, who married the Sister of my Father['s] Mother. – He had an independent fortune and painted merely for his Amusement. – He is said to have had a particular art of extracting Colors out of the Natural Flowers; and some of the Plants and Flowers contained in this Volume are painted with those Colors. This secret, though left behind him, died with those to whom he intrusted it. – He lived many years in great friendship with D[r] Compton Bishop of London and died in his Palace at Fulham; where he planted several Cedars of Libanus (still growing there) and raised many other Exotics from America & Other Countries, the first that are known to have been raised in this Island. – After his Decease Five hundred Pounds were offered‡ by the Ambassador of France for his Master Louis XIV.‡ and refused for this Volume by his Widow, who by her Will left it – with several of his Works and Valuable Curiosities – to my Father Doctor Robert Freind.

The Book contains One hundred Sixty four leaves, paged; Three of which are missing, viz.

Pag.39 containing Three Tulips. [see Insects II, f.60]

153 cont[g] a *Guernsey Lilly*, which was cutt out of a Book by a Lady of great Rank at Chelsea, to whom my Father had lent it.

158 containing two large Bunches of Blue Grapes, which my Father presented to L.S.

The Rest of the Book is intire, containing as follows.

		Present folio	RL Inventory No.	Page this volume	Paper/vellum type*
1	Eleven Animals in miniature; viz. a Fox, Seven Dogs, Three heads of Dogs.	1	24268		?
2	A Dog. – an Indian Fowl. – Seven Flowers, Crocus, Hepatica, Primrose, &c.	2	24269	21	A
3	Snake and Caterpillar (large as the life) – Sprig of an Orange-Tree. Two red Crocus.	3	24270	25	D
4	Eight Flowers and Sprigs. – Mezereon, Gilded Box, Hyacinth, &c.	4	24271		A
5	Dead Jaye (as big as the life) Seven Flowers, Doub: Blue Hepatica, Crocus &c.	5	24272		A

		Present folio	RL Inventory No.	Page this volume	Paper/vellum type*
6	Seven Flowers. Two Daffodils, Persian Iris, Three blue Hyacinths, Crocus.	6	24273		A
7	A Goldfinch in Miniature (pasted on ye leaf.)	158	24425(c)		
	Narcissus, Gentianella, &c. (six flowers in all).	7	24274	27	A
8	Six Flowers. Dwarf Iris, Fretillary, Anemonie, &c.	8	24275		A
9	Eight Flowers. – Two Jonquils, two Auricula's, Speckled Fretillary, &c.	9	24276		A
10	Six Auricula's.	10	24277		A
11	Six Ditto.	11	24278		A
f.130 12	Three Auricula's – Sprig of a double blossom'd Peach.	12	24279		A
13	Two ditto. – Two Narcissus – The Crown Imperial.	13	24280	31	A
14	Fourteen Auricula's. (variegated Sorts.)	14	24281	33	A
15	Two Ditto. – The White Sea-Daffodill – Blue Hyacinth.	15	24282		C
16	Twelve flowers. D. White Narcissus, Blue Hyacinth, Anemonies, &c.	16	24283		A
17	Persian Lilly, Broad-leaved Moly, &c. (Four flowers.)	17	24284	35	C
18	Eight Flowers. Anemonies, Hyacinth, Violets.	18	24285	39	A
19	Savoy Spiderwort. Two Anemonies. Crocus.	19	24286		A
20	Ten Flowers. – Double White Daffodill. Blue Grape flower, & Anemonies.	20	24287	41	A
21	Scarlet Anemonies &c. (Four flowers, and a Single leaf.)	21	24288		A
22	Three Ditto.	22	24289		A
23	Four Ditto, with a Sprig of Barrenwort.	23	24290		A
24	Two Satyrions, Anemonie, and blue Hyacinth.	24	24281	43	B
25	Bright Scarlet Anemonie, two purple ditto, Two Primroses.	25	24292		A
26	Two Anemonies, Black Fretillary.	26	24293		B
27	Nine Flowers. Two Daffodills, Anemonies, Pancies, &c.	27	24294		A
28	Eight Flowers. White Star of Naples, &c. –	28	24295		A
29	Six Tulips.	29	24296		A
30	Two Ditto. – Pancies, & Daisies. (Six flowers)	30	24297		A
31	Three Ditto. – Doub. Anemonie, White Violet, & Pancie.	31	24298	45	A
32	Four Ditto. – & Virginian Fretillary	32	24299		A

		Present folio	RL Inventory No.	Page this volume	Paper/vellum type*
33	Two Ditto. – Black Fretillary, Green Anemonie, &c. (Six flowers)	33	24300		A
34	Four Ditto. – Two yellow Ranunculus, Pancie on the Ground.	34	24301		A
35	Three Ditto. – Narcissus and Jonquil.	35	24302		A
36	One Dº Large. – White Candia Ranunculus, Purple Milkwort	36	24303		A
37	One Ditto. – Blue Iris, Sprig of Syringa. – A Minor Fish (pasted on)	37 158	24304 24425(b)		A
38	One Ditto. – Honeysuckle, Yellow Poppy. – A Golden Minr. Fish. (Do)	38	24305	47	A
40	One Ditto. – Lilly of the Valley, Doub: Wall-flower	39	24306		?
41	Two Ditto. & an Anemony – An Indian Bird with two Perch, (in miniature)	40 158	24307 24425(d)		A
42	Two Ditto. with a Sprig of Striped Hyssop	41	24308		A
43	Three Ditto, (bright Yellow & Red)	42	243090	49	?
44	Three Ditto. Two doub: Narcissus, and a Single Gilli flower.	43	24310		A
45	Two Ditto, & a Crocus.	44	24311		A
46	Two Ditto. White Striped. – Small Wild Red Geranium.	45	24312		A
47	One Dº Purple. – Sprig of a Wild Rose.	46	24313		A
48	One Dº with Red Stripes and a leaf dº springing from it. – A field Pea. – Sprig of Persian Jasmine.	47	24314		A
49	One Dº with a green leaf. – Orange Marigold – Wild Vetch.	48	24315		A
f.131 50	Three Tulips White Striped. – Green Parrot in miniature, pasted on.–	49	24316		B
51	One Ditto. – Great Blue-bottle – Everlasting Tare. –	50	24317	–	B
52	Two Ditto. – Sprig of Rosemary. –	51	24318		A
53	Two Ditto. – The Wild White Sea-pink. –	52	24319		?
54	Two Ditto. – Small Canterbury Bells. – Green Parrot Miniatr. pasted on.	53	24320		B
55	One Ditto. purple striped – Single Marygold, Small Bind-Weed, Red.	54	24321		B
56	Two Ditto (one Red & White, ye Other Yellow) – Gray Parrot in Miniatr. pasted on.	55	24322		A
57	Six Flowers, large Mothe at bottom. Two Tulips, two Ranunculs, Purple Geranium, &c.	56	24323	51	A

		Present folio	RL Inventory No.	Page this volume	Paper/vellum type*
58	Two Speckled Tulips. – Flower of the Horse Chesnut, – Sprig of Arbor Judas	Missing			
59	White Starr-flower – Doub: Red Batchelors Buttons – Doub: White Ladies Violet.	57	24324		B
60	Five flowers. – Large Turky Iris, Asiatic Red Ranunculus, Honeywort &c. – Two Insects.	58	24325		?
61	Six Flowers, and a spotted Moth at bottom. – Ladies Slipper, Columbines various, &c.	59	24326	55	A
62	Five double Columbines, purple &c., Two Duke Cherries.	60	24327		A
63	Variegated Iris, Two Doub: Stocks. – Caterpillar & an Egg –	61	24328		A
64	D^o^ – Blue Convolvulus min^r^, Blue Monkshood with a Butterfly upon it, Upright Willow-flower.	62	24329		A
65	Two Blue Flag-Flowers, – Ranunculus Red, D^o^ yellow, Two Wild Hyacinths, or Harebells	63	24330		A
66	Yellow Iris, Two D^o^ White variegated, Two purple Geraniums, small Ranuncul.	64	24331		A
67	Three Iris^s^, – 2 Lillys of the Valley *Red*, Auricila Red & Yellow. (Six flowers)	65	24332		A
68	Two Ditto. Three Flos Adonis, Velvet striped Anemony, Branched Aspodill. (seven flowers)	66	24333		?
69	Two D^o^ – French Corn-flag Red, Two Sprigs of African Marygold.	67	24334		A
70	The Chinese Iris, Rose-Campion Red, D^o^ variegated with ye Small Blue Dragon-fly upon it. The Satin-flower, the Bee-flower, Amaradulcis, &c. (seven Flow^rs^)A snail, & a Beetle. – A Guinea Hen in Miniature.	68	24335		A
71	Remarkable Double Variegated Iris, Sweet William, African Vetch.	69	24336		D
72	Great Blue Striped Iris, Childing Daisey, a Curious kind of Sedum.	70	24337		A
73	Small Iris of Clusius, Everlast^g^ Pea, Candia Mustard.	71	24338	59	A
74	Fine Striped Ranunculus, Burrage-flowerd Comfrey, Red Wild Campion, Double Cherry.	72	24339		A
75	Tulip (two of its leaves fallen on ye ground) Two pionies, Striped Ranunculus.	73	24340		A
76	Three Red Pionies, Blue Geranium.	74	24341	61	A
77	Two large Double Pionies – The Red and the Blush.	75	24342		A
78	Five Flowers. Guelder Rose with Moth & Caterpillar on ye leaf, Austrian Rose, Featherd Hyacinth, &c. –	76	24343		A

		Present folio	RL Inventory No.	Page this volume	Paper/vellum type*
79	Two Spiderworts (Snail upon One) Two Fennel Flowers, three Roses.	77	24344	63	A
80	Four Roses (the Austrº with leaves fallen) – Brook lime, & Pimpernelle.	78	24345		A
81	Sprig of Roses. Snake with a Caterpillar.	79	24346		A
82	Two Ditto. – Small Sprig of Striped Geranium.	II,80	24347		A
83	Two Ditto, white, & yellow. – Sprig of Small Rampion.	81	24348	67	A
84	Three Ditto, the White Francfort & Cinnamon.	82	24349		B
85	One Dº York & Lancastr – Yellow Jasmine, Field Scabius.	83	24350		A
f.132 86	Sprig of Roses, Indian Scabius, Egyptian Vetch.	84	24351		A
87	Sprig of Provence Dº – Ground Ivy.	85	24352		A
88	Dº with one upon the Ground. – Water Scorpion Grass Blue, or Brook lime.	86	24353		B
89	Two Ditto.	87	24354	69	B
90	One Dº Brabant. Yellow Lupine, White Lupine.	Missing			
91	One Dº variegated. Striped Rose Campion, Coventry Bells.	88	24355	71	B
92	One Dº small red, Canterb: Bells, Afric. Marigold, & three Others. – Green Parrot Peacock, Magpye, & three othr Birds in Miniature.	89	24356		?
93	One Dº – and a Bud. (Red Marble) – Red Martagon with a Caterpillr & three Others.	90	24357		A
94	One Dº – Doub: Larkspur – 2 Nasturtiums – Carnation on ye Ground.	91	24358	75	A
95	One Dº – Larkspur, & Poppie, (single) Borage. – Two Butterflies.	92	24359		A
96	One Dº Red Provence. – Red Lilly, and Two Other Plants.	93	24360		A
97	Spring of Rose buds, Two Blue-Bells, Lilly, Upright Larkspur & Another.	94	24361		A
98	Great Orange Lilly, Small blue-Bell.	95	24362		A
99	Double Yellow Lilly, White Double May-Weed Meadow Blue-Bell.	96	24363		A
100	Large White Lilly, Red Spinach and Another.	97	24364		A
101	Day Lilly, Tode Flax, Malva horaria.	98	24365	77	A
102	Doub: Red Rose Campion, Single Spotted Dº, Larkspur with leaves dropt on ye Ground.	99	24366		A
103	Double Scarlet Lychnis, Doub: Larkspur Rose colrd Sprig of Nutmeg Peaches.	100	24367		A

		Present folio	RL Inventory No.	Page this volume	Paper/vellum type*
104	Single Ditto. and Three Others, field flowers.	101	24368		B
105	Doub: March Marygold, Red Sattin-flower, Sanicle, Two views of a green Caterpillar.	102	24369	81	A
106	Peach-leaved Campanula, Scarlet-Bean, Scabius.	103	24370		A
107	Sprig of Honeysuckle, large Blue Lupin, Two oth.r plants, Stag Fly. – Monkey, & Grey Parrot in Miniature.	104	24371		A
108	Spanish Malva, Nasturtium, Succory and Two Others.	105	24372	83	A
109	Hollihock Doub: Rose Color.d – French and African Marigold.	106	24373		A
110	Six flowers. – Two Carnations, Cornbottles, Scabius, &c.	107	24374		A
111	Three Carnations, Two Sprigs of Gooseberries, Clematitis, Candia Geranium.	108	24375		A
112	Two – and Two Sprigs of D.o – Virginian Silk, Male Pimpernell.	109	24376		A
113	One large Sprig of D.o – Two Fennel Flowers, Damascen Plumbs. – a Locust, & a Silk Worm.	110	24377		A
+	Sprig of Roses on the Blue Paper between this leaf and 114.	156	24423		A
114	Two Ditto, single, Sprig of Oleander, Catherine Pear, Filbert, Caterpillar & its Nymph. – Two Rabbits and a Bird Miniature.	111	24378		A
115	One Sprig D.o – Doub: Larkspur, Convolvulus major, Spanish Broom, Yellow Succory.	112	24379		A
116	Two Ditto. – Red Martagon	113	24380		A
117	One Ditto. – Double Gillyflower, Three Apricots.	114	24381		A
118	One Ditto. – Sprig of Lavender, Sanicle.	115	24382		A
119	Two Ditto. – a green Caterpillar.	116	24383		A
120	Two Ditto. – Two blue Plumbs on a Spray.	117	24384		A
121	Three Ditto with Two buds, single. – Sprig of Dutch Gooseberries.	118	24385	87	A
122	Three Ditto, Single.	Missing			
f.133 123	Two Carnations, a 3.d in bud. – An Indian Virginian Blue-Bird upon a Cucumber	119	24586		A
124	Five Ditto. –	120	24387		A
125	Three Ditto. – Red Valerian flower. –	121	24388		A
126	Three Ditto. –	122	24389		A
127	Five Ditto. –	123	24390		B
128	Five Ditto. –	124	24391		B

		Present folio	RL Inventory No.	Page this volume	Paper/vellum type*
+	Four Carnations on the Blue Paper between Pag. 128 & 129. –	Missing		[E]	
129	Three Ditto. –	125	24392		B
130	Two Ditto. – Sweet William. –	126	24393		B
131	One D°. a Sprig – Sprig of Painted-Lady Pink, & of White Jasmine. –	127	24394		A
132	Three Ditto. – Bunch of the large Blue Grape. –	128	24394		A
133	Golden Mouse-Ear, Small Centaury, Common Bramble in Blossom.	129	24396	89	B
134	Lily-Daffodill of Virginia. – Black Henbane, – Wild Crimson Vetch. –	130	24397	91	C
135	Wild Red Poppy, Greek Valerian, Bastard Nigella.	131	24398	95	B
136	Wild Ragged Robin, Water Gladiolus, March Trefoile.	132	24399	97	C
137	Sagittaria Major, Vipers Buglosse –	133	24400		C
138	Yellow Water-Lilly, – Black Knap-weed.	134	24401		C
139	Scarlet Cardinal Flower, – Two Marygolds.	135	24402		A
140	Five Moth-Mulleins of different Colors. – Purple Snap-Dragon	136	24403		A
141	Large Sun-flower. – Liver-colord Dog in miniature.	137	24404		A
142	Smaller Ditto. – Porcupine, Rabbet, Guinea-Pig, Two Ducks, & Goldfinch in Miniature.	138	24405	103	A
143	Sprig of Red Currants, Sultan-flower, St. Johns-Wort.	139	24406	101	A
144	Sprig of Mulberries with a Spider & Fly in its Webb, – Pimpernell. – Span: Dog, 2 Partridges, and a Viper, in Miniature	140	24407		A
145	Fennel with a Caterpillar & its Nymph. – Sow-bread leaf, with D°. – Cray-fish, Dragon-fly, & Waspe; Two Macau's, Two Dogs, & a Hawk, in Miniature.	141	24408		A
146	Virginian Martagon, Virginian Climber, Ivy-leav'd Sowbread, Cyclamens, Green Caterpillar on a Stalk, Brown Nymph of D°.	142	24409		
—	Man seated for shaving – on y[e] Blue Leaf between 146 and 147 Pages.	Missing		[E]	
147	Passion Flower, Sensitive Plant in a Garden-pot, Meadow-flower, 2 Caterpillars &c.	143	24410	105	A
148	Scarlet Coluthea with a pod dropt off, Blue Cardinal-flower, Bean-Caper.	144	24411		B
149	Pomgranate Flower, Parsley Grape, Crocus with a Caterpillar, Frog & Caterpillar. Onocraterus on Indian Bird. – Monkey eating Cherries, Macaw & Stork in Miniature.	145	24412		A
150	Pepper plant, Ginger, Clary. – (Pepper-pod on the Ground.)	146	24413	107	D

		Present folio	RL Inventory No.	Page this volume	Paper/vellum type*
151	Marvel of Peru, Double Striped Colchicum.	147	24414		A
152	Ditto. – Ditto. – Italian Starwort.	148	24415		A
[153	lacking]				
154	Indian flowering Cane, White Oxeye, Small Wild Vetch.	149	24416		B
155	Amaranthus – the Gold, Scarlet and Peach	Missing			
+	Two men, One carrying part of the Cross from a Print of Reubens between 155, & 156 Pages.	155	24422		E
156	Amaranth.s Tricolor, – An Egyptian Melon.	150	24417		?
157	Foreign Flower (without a name) – Goats-Rue, Small Trefoile (Yellow)	151	24418	109	B
f.134 [158	lacking]				
159	Winter Cherry (Alka Kengi.) – Winter Daffodill, Saffron. – Mexico Monkey in Miniature	152	24419	113	A
160	Solomons Seal, Filius ante Patrem, Another Small Plant.	153	24420	117	D
161	Sprig of the Arbutus with its fruit. – Two Ducks in miniature pasted on.	154	24421		A
162	Dunghill Cock – Dead Partridge – dead Bullfinch.	158 159	24425(a) 24426(c)		F F
163	Bunch of Green Grapes – Sprig of Huntbois Strawberries – D.o of Cherries.	158 157 157	24425(e) 24424(a) 24424(c)		F F F
164	Two oysters (one opened), Sprig of Medlar. Three with fruit, Three Walnuts (one crackt).	159 157 159	24426(b) 24424(b) 24426(a)		F F F